Fodor's
25 Best

NEW YORK CITY

Contents

KEY TO SYMBOLS

- ✚ Map reference to the accompanying pull-out map
- ✉ Address
- ☎ Telephone number
- ◉ Opening/closing times

- 🍴 Restaurant or café
- Ⓜ Nearest subway (Metro) station
- ▣ Nearest bus route
- 🚆 Nearest rail station

ENTERTAINMENT 126

Whether you're after a cultural fix or just want a place to relax with a drink after a hard day's sightseeing, we've made the best choices for you.

EAT 138

Uncover great dining experiences, from a quick bite for lunch to top-notch evening meals.

SLEEP 150

We've brought together the best hotels in the city, whatever budget you're on.

NEED TO KNOW 160

The practical information you need to make your trip run smoothly.

PULL-OUT MAP

The pull-out map with this book is a comprehensive street plan of the city, with a more detailed map of Central Park on the back. We've given grid references within the book for each sight and listing.

🛥 Nearest riverboat or ferry stop

♿ Facilities for visitors with disabilities

🛈 Tourist information

❷ Other practical information

🅱 Admission charges: Expensive ($20 and over), Moderate ($11–$19) and Inexpensive (under $10)

▷ Further information

Introducing New York

"New York is an island off the coast of Europe." There's a lot of truth in this witticism, and it's no wonder this is the US city most overseas visitors choose first. The qualities that weld New Yorkers to the city also distinguish them from most Americans.

Residents of Manhattan, the most densely populated of New York City's boroughs, value directness, diversity and creativity; they live at a ridiculous pace; they work all hours (they have to, to pay the rent); they walk—fast—everywhere; they fail to keep their opinions to themselves; they are street smart; they are capital L Liberal. New York is a key Blue State, having voted Democrat in the last eight presidential elections, turning out in large numbers against native son Donald Trump. The city that actually lived through the horror of the 9/11 attack refuses to give in to fear; New Yorkers have all the chutzpah they ever did.

In New York, change is the only constant. The crime-ridden, graffiti-scarred mean streets of the late 20th century are all but a distant memory. In fact, these days New York is the safest large city in America (at least according to the NYPD). In stark contrast to the gritty days, you'll see strollers wherever you go, because there is a mini baby-boom in progress. Real-estate prices are in the realm of fiction, and a whole lot of regular folks have decamped for Brooklyn, while those who can't afford Brooklyn have gone to Queens. These days parts of Harlem are glamorous and beautiful; the Bronx is next. Staten Island, the fifth borough, which most visitors know only for its ferry, is the final frontier.

For many, Manhattan will always be the center of the universe. It's where deals are done, stars are born, legends—and fortunes—are made. Nowhere else in America offers such diversity in fashion, food, design, theater and the arts. The constant stimulation is addictive, and simply being here is worth a thousand inconveniences. You can take in only so much of the big picture in one visit. So do as New Yorkers do—find a corner of the city and make it your own.

FACTS AND FIGURES

- Visitors in 2018: 65.2 million (the ninth straight year that numbers have gone up)
- Dollars spent by visitors in 2017: $44 billion
- Hotel rooms by end of 2019: 122,600
- Population in 2018: 8.61 million
- Licensed yellow cabs: 13,587
- Feature films shot in New York: 28 in 2018 (and 18 TV series in 2018)

REAL ESTATE

New York is in the midst of a building boom, with luxury skyscrapers that are among the tallest—and most expensive—in the world. This has put the squeeze on some middle-class New Yorkers. Still, many residents view their homes as not just their castles, but also as their portfolio, their retirement plan and their chief financial burden.

BROOKLYN

Once a separate city, the vast borough of Brooklyn across the East River has experienced a migration of disaffected Manhattanites that has changed its character forever. Previously, Brooklyn wasn't fashionable; now it's a destination for excellent restaurants, music venues, avant-garde theater and great parties in those oh-so-desirable brownstones.

ONE WORLD TRADE CENTER

Nicknamed the Freedom Tower, the new tower in the World Trade Center (▷ 62–63) is officially called One World Trade Center (1WTC). It stands 1,776ft (541m) high—symbolic of the date of US independence—making it the tallest building in America. The stunning observatory opened to the public in spring 2015.

Focus On Architecture

New York is constantly changing and nowhere is this more apparent than in its architecture. Skyscrapers symbolize the city, but it has many other gems, from Beaux Arts beauties to art deco designs. As you tour the city, watch for the parade of great buildings spanning the years.

The Battery to City Hall

A sample of old and new New York is found downtown, where the city began. The Continental Congress dined in 1774 at Fraunces Tavern (▷ 79), now part dining, part museum. St. Paul's Chapel (1776, ▷ 72) is the city's oldest, while the Gothic spires of Trinity Church (▷ 59), completed in 1846, were the city's tallest for 50 years. The restored Corbin Building (13 John Street/ Broadway, 1888–89) was a pioneer skyscraper. 195 Broadway, once the AT&T building (1912–23), is notable for its many columns, inside and out. Architect Cass Gilbert was responsible for two sites marking changing tastes: the Beaux Arts US Custom House (1907, ▷ 73), and the Gothic-inspired, terra-cotta-sheathed Woolworth Building (233 Broadway, 1913). It was the world's tallest until 1930.

The towers grew so thick and fast that the streets of the Financial District became virtual canyons, despite laws passed in 1916 to allow light to reach ground level. The race to claim the "tallest" title has bounced between downtown and midtown. One World Trade Center (2014, ▷ 62–63) is the current champion.

Civic Center

New York's finest early building is City Hall (1802–1812, ▷ 67), a French Renaissance-Federal blend with lavish interiors. The tiled vaults and triumphal arch of the nearby Municipal Building (1907, 1 Center Street), are also notable.

Clockwise from top left: Norman Foster's Hearst Tower; the triangular Flatiron Building; 19th-century Gramercy Park Historic District; interior of the US Custom House,

Midtown

While Midtown has Beaux Arts classics like The New York Public Library (1911, ▷ 48–49) and Grand Central Terminal (1913, ▷ 34–35), by the 1930s art deco was the rage. Greats like Rockefeller Center (▷ 50–51), the Chrysler Building (▷ 67) and the Empire State Building (▷ 28–29) often topped the tallest list. Lever House (1952, 90 Park Avenue) ushered in the era of glass-walled skyscrapers such as Mies Van der Rohe's 1958 Seagram Building (375 Park Avenue). Later came the Time Warner Towers on Columbus Circle (2003) and the Hearst Tower (2006, 300 West 57th Street)

Today's buildings are growing taller and slimmer. Two giants due for completion in 2020 on West 57th Street are no. 111, an 82-story residence said to be the thinnest in the world, and no. 225, the world's highest residential building at 131 stories.

More Highlights

On the Upper West Side (▷ 102) are the landmark apartment buildings of Central Park West and Broadway and side streets of classic New York brownstones. Fifth Avenue on the Upper East Side (▷ 96) has the Metropolitan Museum and several Beaux Arts mansions-turned-museums plus Frank Lloyd Wright's spiraling Guggenheim Museum (▷ 38–39). SoHo's Cast Iron district is distinctive (▷ 52–53), as are the townhouses of Greenwich Village (▷ 36–37).

Architectural guides and tours

For more details on New York's architecture, see the *American Institute of Architects Guide to New York City* (2010) and *New York City Landmarks* (2015). The Metropolitan Art Society (mas.org) offers numerous guided architecture walks, as well as a guidebook, *10 Architectural Walks in Manhattan* (2009).

one of New York's finest Beaux Arts buildings; The Row, Washington Square North; the spire of the Chrysler Building; the Woolworth Building's neo-Gothic facade

INTRODUCING NEW YORK

7

Top Tips For...

These great suggestions will help you tailor your ideal visit to New York, no matter how you choose to spend your time.

Star Chefs
Jean-Georges Vongerichten's restaurant, at 1 Central Park (▷ 145), is the flagship of his ever-growing worldwide empire.
Daniel Boulud at **Café Boulud** will wow you (▷ 143). Save room for the desserts.
At **Eleven Madison Park** (▷ 144), chef Daniel Humm is a master of reinvention, with the most complex tasting menus in the city.
For superb fish, few match Eric Ripert at **Le Bernardin** (▷ 142).

Being On Trend
Head on over to **Jeffrey New York** (▷ 122) to refresh your wardrobe, or, for vintage, head to **Resurrection** (▷ 125).
Get a taste of the LES (Lower East Side) music vibe at the **Parkside Lounge** (▷ 136).
Check out the latest art show at the **New Museum** (▷ 70) or go gallery hopping in **Chelsea** (▷ 67).
Blossom on Columbus (▷ 143) serves delicious vegan fare.

Partying till Dawn
On Friday and Saturday, dance the night away to live Latin music at **SOB's** (▷ 137).
Go with the groove at the late-night jazz series at the **Blue Note** (▷ 132) from 12.30am on Friday and Saturday.
Ward off a hangover with a hearty breakfast or some Ukrainian soul food at cozy **Veselka** (▷ 149), open 24 hours.

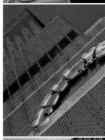

Big and Beautiful Views
Take in the lake view from Central Park's **Loeb Boathouse** (▷ 146).
See the city lights from a rooftop bar (▷ 131, panel).

Clockwise from top left: Vintage style for sale; view from the Top of the Rock at the Rockefeller Center; tiger enclosure at the Bronx Zoo; head to the Blue Note for

Top of the Rock (▷ 51), at the Rockefeller Center, rivals the **Empire State Building** (▷ 28–29) for views, but the **One World Observatory** (▷ 63) is the city's highest—you can see 50 miles (80km) on a clear day.

Bringing the Kids
You can never go wrong with a good zoo. **Bronx Zoo** (▷ 74) is vast; the one in **Central Park** (▷ 18–19) won't take all day. Take them to **Serendipity 3** (▷ 147, panel) for frozen hot chocolate.
Get tickets for a family-friendly show at **The New Victory Theater** (▷ 135).
You could spend days exploring the **American Museum of Natural History** (▷ 14–15), from its dinosaur halls and Hall of Gems to the Space Theater.

Classic NYC
Bergdorf's, Bloomingdale's, Macy's and Saks are classic department stores with different personalities (▷ 120, 123, 125).
The stunning **Chrysler Building** (▷ 67) is New York's favorite skyscraper and an art deco masterpiece.
Walk across the **Brooklyn Bridge** (▷ 66–67). Take in the scenic view on a free ride on the **Staten Island ferry** (▷ 108).

Sporting Pursuits
If you are here during baseball season (April to September), **Yankee Stadium** (▷ 75) is a must. Or catch the Mets at Citi Field.
Madison Square Garden (▷ 135) has it all: basketball (the Knicks), boxing, tennis, track and field, hockey, dog shows and more.
There's a game of something in progress in **Central Park** (▷ 18–19) all summer long. If it's winter, you can go skating at the **Wollman Rink**.
Brooklyn's **Barclays Center** is home to both basketball and hockey (620 Atlantic Avenue).

late-night jazz; the pedestrian walkway, Brooklyn Bridge; Madison Square Garden; the New Museum; Café Boulud, bastion of fine cuisine

Timeline

Pre-1600 Native American groups populate New York area.

1609 Henry Hudson sails up the Hudson River seeking the Northwest Passage.

1625 "Nieuw Amsterdam" is founded by the Dutch West India Company on the tip of Manhattan Island. The following year the colony's leader purchases the island from the Native Americans for 60 guilders in trade goods.

THE FIGHT FOR INDEPENDENCE

In 1664, Wall Street's wall failed to deter the British, who invaded Manhattan Island and named it New York. The first rumblings of Revolution came in 1765, when Stamp Act protesters rallied in Bowling Green Park. In 1770, the Sons of Liberty fought the British at the Battle of Golden Hill and, in 1776, the American Revolutionary War began and the British chose New York as their headquarters. The Declaration of Independence was read at City Hall Park in July 1776 and the Treaty of Paris ended the war in 1783.

1664 In a bloodless coup, the British take over and rename the island New York.

1776 American Revolutionary War begins.

1785 New York becomes the capital of the United States (until 1790).

1789 George Washington is sworn in as first US president at Federal Hall.

1827 Slavery in New York is abolished.

1845 Start of the first great wave of immigrants after the Irish Potato Famine.

1863 Civil War Draft Riots divide the city.

1868 The city's first "El" (elevated train) opens.

1886 The Statue of Liberty is officially unveiled.

Inauguration of George Washington on the balcony of Federal Hall in 1789

Immigrants arriving in New York Harbor, 1892

1892 Ellis Island immigration center opens.

1904 The first subway opens.

1929 The Great Depression follows the Wall Street Crash.

1933 Prohibition ends after 14 years. Fiorello LaGuardia becomes mayor.

1954 Ellis Island is closed down.

1964 Race riots erupt in Harlem and Brooklyn.

1975 A federal loan saves New York City from bankruptcy.

1990 David Dinkins, New York's first black mayor, takes office.

2001 Terrorists fly two hijacked planes into the World Trade Center, killing nearly 3,000 people.

2011 The National September 11 Memorial opens at the World Trade Center Site.

2013 The new tower at One World Trade Center becomes the tallest skyscraper in America.

2017 More than 400,000 people jam the streets as part of a nation-wide Women's March in January.

2019 The Shed, the city's newest performing arts venue, opens as part of Hudson Yards, a massive new business and cultural center.

TENEMENT LIFE

As you make your first explorations in New York, consider how it was for the early immigrants, especially those who were herded through Ellis Island, then crammed into Lower East Side tenements. By the end of the 19th century, the immigrant neighborhoods were dominated by Italians and Eastern European Jews and was the most densely populated place on earth. Many of these immigrants became garment workers in the ornate cast-iron buildings of SoHo, though many also sewed clothes at their overcrowded homes. Find out more at the Tenement Museum (▷ 72).

Handouts during the Great Depression, following the Wall Street Crash of 1929

The Tenement Museum

★ Top 25

This section contains the must-see Top 25 sights and experiences in New York. They are listed alphabetically, and numbered so you can locate them on the inside front cover.

TOP 25

1 American Museum of Natural History

HIGHLIGHTS

- Blue whale
- Titanosaur
- Cape York meteorite
- Dinosaur halls
- Journey to the Stars
- Star of India
- Animal dioramas
- Dinosaur embryo
- IMAX theater shows

TIP

● You can observe the entire life cycle of tropical butterflies from October to June at the Butterfly Conservatory.

Of the 36 million items owned by the American Museum of Natural History—the largest such institution in the world—only a small fraction is on show. Don't miss the renowned dinosaur halls and stunning animal dioramas in native habitats.

Star attractions The original museum building opened in 1877 and, as it grew, its facade sported pink brownstone and granite towers, turrets and a grand Beaux Arts entrance on Central Park West. This opens into a soaring rotunda containing the museum's beloved Barosaurus, and visitors soon encounter the museum's prized Titanosaur cast (so enormous that its head extends into the hallway). The museum is best known for its splendid dinosaur halls, where real fossil specimens

From left: The magnificent rotunda of the American Museum of Natural History is dominated by the skeleton of a Barosaurus; the stunning Rose Center for Earth and Space, adjoining the museum, includes the Hayden Planetarium, where space shows take place

(rather than models) of an Apatosaurus and the first Tyrannosaurus rex ever exhibited are displayed. Another highlight is the enormous model of a blue whale looming over the Hall of Ocean Life. There will be new exhibits and more access to collections when the Gilder Center, a major addition, is completed in 2022.

Gems and more The 563-carat Star of India sapphire is part of the Morgan Memorial Hall of Gems, which contains merely a fraction of the museum's precious stones. There's far too much to see in one day, with four city blocks and the entire evolution of life on Earth covered. In the adjoining Rose Center for Earth and Space, a giant sphere contains the Big Bang Theater and the Hayden Planetarium, where thrilling space shows are projected on the dome.

THE BASICS

amnh.org
🛨 C6
✉ Central Park West/ 79th Street
☎ 212/769-5100
🕐 Daily 10–5.45
🍴 Various
🚇 B, C 81st Street– Museum of Natural History
🚌 M7, M10, M11, M79, M86
♿ Good
💲 Expensive
❓ 1-hour tours from 10.15 until 3.15. Call 212/769-5200 for advance reservations for special exhibits and events, such as occasional sleepovers (some for children, others for adults only)

HIGHLIGHTS

● Williamsburg
● Brooklyn Heights Promenade
● Bandshell concerts
● The Brooklyn Academy of Music (BAM)
● Brooklyn Museum of Art
● Brooklyn Bridge Park

TIP

● Brooklyn Academy (BAM.org) and St. Ann's Warehouse (stannsware house.org) in Brooklyn offer some of New York's best avant-garde theater.

Brooklyn has it all—one of the largest art museums in the US and some of New York's best restaurants; beaches and a park; a zoo, aquarium and children's museum; stylish neighborhoods and avant-garde arts.

Big, bigger, biggest If Brooklyn were still a separate city, it would be the fourth largest in the US. Home to more than 2.6 million people, it is the most populous of New York's boroughs, with Russian, Middle Eastern, Italian, West Indian, Hasidic Jewish and Chinese neighborhoods. The Brooklyn Museum, one of the largest in the US, has collections ranging from pre-Columbian art to 58 Rodin sculptures, plus what many feel are the best Egyptian rooms outside Egypt and the British Museum. Its newly renovated, and now even larger,

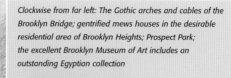

Clockwise from far left: The Gothic arches and cables of the Brooklyn Bridge; gentrified mews houses in the desirable residential area of Brooklyn Heights; Prospect Park; the excellent Brooklyn Museum of Art includes an outstanding Egyptian collection

"Art of Korea" Gallery has a renowned collection of Korean art. Steps from the museum's grand entrance is the Brooklyn Botanic Garden. Then, farther south, wander in Prospect Park, where summertime events and the zoo are highlights.

The bridge and beyond Brooklyn Bridge Park is an 85-acre (34ha) greenway reclaimed from derelict piers along the Brooklyn Heights waterfront, with jogging paths, water sports and outdoor festivals. From Brooklyn Heights, you can climb stairs to the Brooklyn Bridge pedestrian crossing or visit the Promenade for its view of Manhattan. Williamsburg is among the trendiest spots, known for its restaurants, clubs, artisanal foods and crafts and, in warm weather, the renowned Brooklyn Flea's Smorgasburg artisanal food market in an outdoor setting.

THE BASICS

Brooklyn Heights
➕ H22
🚇 2, 3 Clark Street

Brooklyn Museum
brooklynmuseum.org
➕ See map ▷ 110
✉ 200 Eastern Parkway
☎ 718/638-5000
🕐 Wed, Fri–Sun 11–6, Thu 11–10
🚇 2, 3 Eastern Parkway–Brooklyn Museum
💰 Moderate

Prospect Park
prospectpark.org
➕ See map ▷ 110
☎ 718/965-8951
🚇 2, 3 Grand Army Plaza Station; F 15th Street–Prospect Park

Williamsburg
➕ See map ▷ 111

Brooklyn Flea's Smorgasburg
smorgasburg.com
✉ Saturday: East River State Park, 90 Kent Avenue. Sunday: Prospect Park–Breeze Hill. Summer months only; check website for details

Take the Ferry
Ferries sail from Manhattan to Brooklyn. Visit ferry.nyc for more information

HIGHLIGHTS

- Delacorte Theater, Shakespeare in the Park
- Belvedere Castle
- Conservatory Water
- Bethesda Fountain
- Wollman Rink in winter
- Heckscher Playground
- Swedish Cottage Marionette Theatre
- Walking in the Ramble

TIPS

- Don't walk alone in isolated areas at night.
- Watch out for bicycles on the roads.

The park is the escape valve for the city. Without it New York would overheat—especially during the summer, when the temperature rises. Bikers, runners, dog walkers and frisbee players convene here. It's a way of life.

The Greensward Plan In the mid-19th century, when few lived in Manhattan north of 42nd Street, *New York Evening Post* editor William Cullen Bryant campaigned until the city invested $5 million in 843 acres (340ha) of undeveloped land. Responsible for clearing the land was journalist Frederick Law Olmsted, who, with English architect Calvert Vaux, also won the competition to design the park with his "Greensward Plan." Five million cubic tons of dirt were cleared to create this green space.

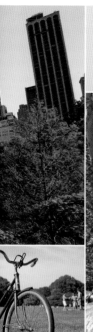

Clockwise from left: The Pond, at the south end of Central Park; a bronze statue depicting characters in Lewis Carroll's Alice in Wonderland, just north of the Conservatory Water; Sheep Meadow, a great place to relax; the tribute to John Lennon in Strawberry Fields

Fun and games Start at the Dairy Visitor Center and pick up a map and events list. These show the layout of the park and tell you about the Wildlife Conservation Center (Zoo), the Carousel, the playgrounds, rinks, fountains, statues and Strawberry Fields, where John Lennon is commemorated close to the Dakota Building, where he lived and was shot. But the busy life of the park is not recorded on maps: making music on the Mall; sunbathing in Sheep Meadow; admiring the view from Belvedere Castle; Great Lawn softball leagues; doing the loop road by bike; sailing toy boats on the Conservatory Water; bird-watching in the Ramble; jogging around the Reservoir; rowing on the Lake; fishing at Harlem Meer; and bouldering on the outcrops of Manhattan schist (rock).

THE BASICS

centralparknyc.org

➕ D2–D9 (see reverse of sheet map)

☎ 212/310-6600

🕐 Dairy Visitor Center, 65th Street, daily 9–7 Jun–Aug, 10–5 Sep–May; other kiosks throughout the park (212/794-4543)

🍴 Restaurants, kiosks

🚇 A, B, C, D, 1 59th Street–Columbus Circle; N, Q, R, W 57th Street–7th Avenue; N, R, W 5th Avenue–59th Street; F 57th Street; B, D 72nd Street

🚌 M1, M2, M3, M4, M5, M10. Crosstown M66, M72, M79, M86

♿ Moderate

🆓 Free

HIGHLIGHTS

● Mahayana Buddhist
Temple (en.mahayana.us)
✉ 133 Canal Street
🕐 Daily 8.30–5.45
💲 Donation
● Museum of Chinese
in America (▷ 70)
● New Kam Man
(200 Canal Street, ▷ 124)
● Doyers Street
● Columbus Park
(✉ Bayard/Baxter streets)

TIP

● Visit Columbus Park,
where you can see every-
thing from fortune tellers to
tai chi to Chinese singers
and instrumentalists, who
perform near the pavilion
on weekends.

New York's Chinatown has swallowed
nearly all of Little Italy and has spread over
a great deal of the Lower East Side. Wander
here and become immersed by the sights
and sounds of a busy Asian community.

Going west Chinese people first came to
New York in the late 19th century, fleeing
persecution on the west coast. But, by 1880,
some 10,000 men—mostly Cantonese railroad
workers—had settled among the Irish and
Italians of the old Five Points area. The Chinese
Exclusion Act (1883) kept the community small
until immigration restrictions were lifted in
1965. While the first arrivals were mostly
Cantonese speakers, most of today's immigrants are Fujianese. New York has two more
Chinatowns: in Flushing (Queens) and Eighth

Clockwise from left: Columbus Park is at the heart of Manhattan's Chinatown, a long-established Asian enclave and a quiet spot for a Chinese board game; a statue of Confucius; vibrant street stall

Avenue, Brooklyn, with thousands of residents. Manhattan's, though, is the second-largest in the western hemisphere.

A whirl of color Chinatown is the city's most colorful neighborhood, an area bustling day and night with sidewalk vendors, open-air food stalls laden with exotic fruits and vegetables, fragrant bakeries, tea shops, herbalists and restaurants serving fare from dim-sum to gourmet delights. Shopping can mean back scratchers, Chinese slippers or fine art and antiques. Amidst it all, authentic culture still can be found at the quiet Mahayana Buddhist Temple, with its 16ft (4.9m) Buddha, watching tai-chi at Columbus Park or at the Museum of Chinese in America (▷ 70), which tells the story of New York's Chinese community from its birth to today.

THE BASICS
explorechinatown.com
✚ F19–F20
✉ Roughly delineated by Worth Street/East Broadway, the Bowery, Grand Street, Centre Street
🍴 Numerous (some close around 10pm)
🚇 6, J, N, Q, R, Z Canal Street; B, D Grand Street
🚌 M22, M103
♿ Poor
❓ Visitors' Kiosk at Canal and Baxter streets, daily 10–6

5 Cooper Hewitt Smithsonian Design Museum

HIGHLIGHTS

- Original 1903 detailing
- HD touch-screen tables
- Immersion Room
- Process Lab
- Design Triennial
- Summer concerts
- Textile collection

TIP

- The renovated garden is free to the public and is open Mon–Fri 8–6, Sat 10–9, Sun 10–6. The café is also free to visit.

America's national design museum is a marvelous showcase of everything from cutting-edge work by up-and-coming artists to classic examples of fine furnishings and accessories. All of it is housed in one of New York's most stunning mansions.

Carnegie, Cooper and Hewitt The mansion that contains this superb collection belonged to industrialist Andrew Carnegie, who, in 1903, had asked architects Babb, Cook & Willard for "the most modest, plainest and most roomy house in New York City". This he did not receive (aside from the roominess), since this little chateau was built with modern conveniences galore—air-conditioning and elevators—and a big gated garden. The entire neighborhood came to be known as

Clockwise from left: Outside the Cooper Hewitt Smithsonian Design Museum on East 91st Street; the museum's Arthur Ross Terrace and Garden is often used to host art installations and events; the Great Hall inside the museum

Carnegie Hill. Andrew's wife, Louise, lived here until her death in 1946. Twenty years later, the collection of the Hewitt sisters (decorative arts, ceramics, textiles and more), which had been previously exhibited at the Cooper Union (▷ 24), became a part of the Smithsonian and moved into the mansion.

State of the art The museum's recent revamp was designed to make its exhibitions more interactive. In the Immersion Room, you can project textile patterns onto blank walls and then create your own. In the Process Lab, you can make your own protoype or see a 3D printer in action. However, these state-of-the-art exhibits have not displaced the Hewitt sisters' core collection and Carnegie's home is still shown to good effect.

THE BASICS
cooperhewitt.org
✚ E4
✉ 2 E 91st Street
☎ 212/849-8400
🕐 Sun–Fri 10–6, Sat 10–9
🍴 Café
🚇 4, 5, 6 86th Street
🚌 M1, M2, M3, M4
♿ Good
🎟 Moderate (by donation Sat 6–9pm)
❓ Free tours daily

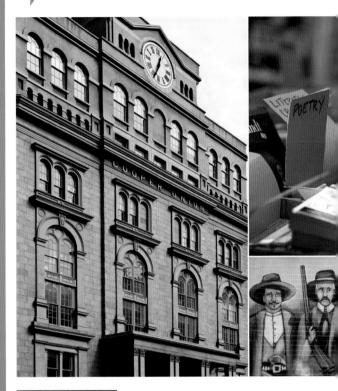

HIGHLIGHTS

● Merchant's House Museum
● Exploring St. Mark's Place
● Diverse array of foods

TIP

● The Strand (▷ 125) on Broadway has 18 miles (29km) of shelves packed with new and used titles. In an area that was once lined with second-hand bookstores, the Strand is one of the few remaining places to find obscure titles.

Once an immigrant neighborhood—and then the rundown bohemia celebrated in the musical *Rent*—the East Village is now prime real estate. Nearby NoHo is quieter and full of historic streets and sites.

Early days What was once Dutch Governor Peter Stuyvesant's farm, or bowery, later became a mostly German enclave. Jews, Poles and Ukrainians followed. Meanwhile, streets such as Bond and Lafayette, in what is today called NoHo (North of Houston), were home to New York's mercantile elite, including John Jacob Astor, the country's richest man.

Historic sites Cooper Union, founded by industrialist Peter Cooper and built in 1859, was the spot where Abraham Lincoln gave his

Clockwise from far left: Cooper Union, an East Village landmark; trading on the area's literary associations; the neighborhood's Ukrainian heritage is celebrated at the Ukrainian Museum; architectural detail inside Grace Church; an East Village mural

landmark "Right Makes Might" anti-slavery speech. The city's second-oldest church, St. Mark's Church-in-the-Bowery, boasts Peter Stuyvesant's grave. On Broadway, Grace Church was the debut of architect James Renwick, who went on to build St. Patrick's Cathedral (▷ 71). The Ukrainian Museum, in the heart of the immigrant neighborhood, features textiles and beautifully decorated Easter eggs. In NoHo, the Merchant's House Museum is an intact early 19th-century home lived in by the same family for nearly a century.

St. Mark's Place The main thoroughfare of the East Village is St. Mark's. In the 1960s, counter-culture exploded along this street, which included Andy Warhol's Electric Circus. Today it is a mix of shops, restaurants and tattoo parlors.

THE BASICS

✚ F16; east of Broadway and south of 14th Street

◎ F, M Lower East Side–2nd Avenue; 6 Astor Place

Ukrainian Museum

ukrainianmuseum.org

✚ F17

✉ 222 E 6th Street/2nd–3rd avenues

☎ 212/228-0110

🕐 Wed–Sun 11.30–5

♿ Good 💲 Moderate

Merchant's House Museum

merchantshouse.org

✚ E17

✉ 29 E 4th Street/Lafayette–Bowery

☎ 212/777-1089

🕐 Thu 12–8, Fri–Mon 12–5; tours at 2pm

♿ Poor 💲 Moderate

HIGHLIGHTS

● Wall of Honor
● Peopling of America galleries
● The American Flag of Faces™

TIP

● To avoid lines and wait times, try to be on the first ferry to Ellis Island at 8.30 (which also serves the Statue of Liberty). The lines to board ferries grow during the day, especially in summer. The last ferry departs at 3.30pm.

Visiting Ellis Island, the gateway to America for millions of immigrants from 1892 to1954, is a poignant reminder of the obstacles so many people had to overcome to reach this country.

Half of all America It was the poor immigrants who docked at Ellis Island, since travelers in first-class passage were given permission to disembark straight into Manhattan. Young Annie Moore, aged 15 and the first immigrant to land at Ellis Island, arrived in 1892. She was followed by some 16 million immigrants over the next 60 years, including such future success stories as Irving Berlin and Frank Capra. Unsurprisingly, around one-third of the current population of the United States can trace their roots to an Ellis Island immigrant.

Clockwise from far left: Exhibition documenting the arrival of early immigrants to New York; statue of Annie Moore, the first immigrant to arrive at Ellis Island; inside the Great Hall; view of Ellis Island from the ferry; the view of Lower Manhattan from Ellis Island; an immigrant's records

Island of Hope, Island of Tears The exhibition in the main building conveys the indignities, frustrations and fears of the immigrants. Choose a ranger-guided tour or the free, 45-minute audio tour which accompanies you around the route that new arrivals took, from the Baggage Room, where people had to abandon all they owned, then onward to the Registry Room and through the inspection chambers, where the medical, mental and political status of each immigrant was ascertained. In the museum, the American Family Immigration History Center® gives access to passenger ship records of millions of immigrants (for a fee). The Peopling of America galleries tell of the hardships and struggles of immigrants in the years before and after the island's processing station.

THE BASICS

nps.gov/elis

✚ See map ▷ 110

✉ Ellis Island

☎ 212/543-3200

🕔 Daily 9.30–5; extended hours in summer

🍴 Café

🚇 4, 5 Bowling Green, 1 South Ferry, then take ferry

🚌 M5, M20, M15 South Ferry, then take the ferry

⛴ Ferry departs Battery Park South Ferry every 30 min. Ferry information: tel 877/523-9849, statuecruises.com

♿ Good

💲 Museum free; ferry expensive

❓ Audio tours

HIGHLIGHTS

- The view at any time of day or night
- Second-floor gallery
- Marble art-deco lobby

TIPS

- Save time (though not the security check) by printing out advance tickets from the website. Express Passes for an extra fee will bypass lines.
- The colored lights at the summit were introduced in 1976 and are changed to mark different events.

It may have lost its crown as the world's tallest building a long time ago, but the Empire State Building remains New York's most famous skyscraper. Views from the observatories are incomparable and a $165 million revamp has made a visit even more rewarding.

Still king It was the world's tallest building when it opened in 1931 after record-fast construction of four stories a week. But the 1930s were the height of the Depression and few could afford to rent space; they called it the Empty State Building. Only visitors to the observatory kept the building solvent and they are still coming: four million visitors each year. The changes unveiled in 2019 included a new entrance to reduce crowding and a second-floor

From left: Head to the 102nd Floor Observatory for panoramic views of New York; there are good views of the Empire State Building itself from 34th Street

gallery that tells the building's dramatic story. A 24ft-high (7m) scale model greets visitors, and makes a great photo opp. To make the inevitable wait a little more pleasant, displays show some of the many celebrity visitors, as well as magazine covers and movie posters that the building has featured on over the years. The exit is through the famous art-deco lobby.

The facts It is 1,454ft (443m) high, with 102 floors. The frame contains 60,000 tons of steel, 10 million bricks line the building, and there are 6,500 windows. The elevator whisks you to the 86th-floor, open-air observation deck in 55 seconds. A new glass elevator travels to the 102nd floor enclosed observatory, where floor-to-ceiling windows provide a 360-degree panorama (an extra ticket is required).

THE BASICS

esbnyc.com
✚ E13
✉ 20 W 34th Street/
5th–6th Avenue
☎ 212/736-3100
🕐 Daily 8am–2am; last admission 1.15am; Sunrise Experience on selected days (100 tickets per day)
🍴 Restaurants
Ⓢ B, D, F, N, Q, R, W 34th Street–Herald Square
🚌 M1, M2, M3, M4, M5
🚉 PATH 34th Street–Avenue of the Americas
♿ Good
💲 Expensive

HIGHLIGHTS

- Shopping!
- Empire State Building
- Rockefeller Center
- The Met
- The Guggenheim
- Cooper Hewitt

TIP

- Try to see a parade—St. Patrick's Day Parade, the biggest, is on March 17.

Fifth Avenue is still the grand old dame of New York shopping, its Midtown section lined with prestigious stores. There's a lot more to see along this 6-mile (10km) thoroughfare though—famous museums, historic mansions and glorious Central Park.

Tradition and invention Fifth Avenue runs all the way from Washington Square Park, up past Central Park, and houses some of the most pricey and notable real estate in New York. Walk along the avenue and you'll pass the Flatiron Building (▷ 68), the Empire State Building (▷ 28–29), the New York Public Library (▷ 48–49), Rockefeller Center (▷ 50–51), St. Patrick's Cathedral (▷ 71), the Frick Collection (▷ 32–33), the Metropolitan Museum of Art (▷ 44–45), the Guggenheim

Clockwise from far left: For most visitors Fifth Avenue is synonymous with shopping; Saks Fifth Avenue, one of New York's most prestigious department stores; designer brands abound; the Cooper Hewitt Smithsonian Design Museum

(▷ 38–39) and the Cooper Hewitt Smithsonian Design Museum (▷ 22–23), just a few of the buildings that represent the development of Fifth Avenue.

Shop, shop, shop Stores along Fifth are generally high end, but window shopping is encouraged. Start with the jewelry emporia of Tiffany & Co. (57th Street) and Cartier (No. 653), the 24-hour Apple Store (▷ 119) or the department stores. Bergdorf Goodman (▷ 120) is at 58th Street and Armani and Gucci are at 56th. Saks Fifth Avenue (▷ 125) has been at 50th Street since 1922. If you plan to shop till you drop, two excellent hotels stand opposite each other on Fifth Avenue and 55th Street: the Peninsula New York and the St. Regis (▷ 159).

THE BASICS

➕ E16–E1

✉ From Washington Square to 143rd Street

🚇 4, 5, 6 (various stops), N, R, W 5th Avenue–59th Street; E, M 5th Avenue–53rd Street

🚌 M1, M2, M3, M4

HIGHLIGHTS

● *St. Jerome*, El Greco (c.1590–1600)
● *Sir Thomas More*, Holbein (1527)
● *Officer and the Laughing Girl*, Vermeer (c.1657)
● *Self Portrait*, Rembrandt (c.1658)
● *The Progress of Love*, Fragonard (1771–72)
● *Philip IV of Spain*, Velázquez (1644)

Industrialist Henry Clay Frick amassed one of the world's greatest collections of 14th- to 19th-century paintings, porcelain, furniture and bronzes. While the 1900s manision that held his treasures is under restoration, the art is at the Breuer.

The man and the mansion Henry Clay Frick (1849–1919) was chairman of the Carnegie Steel Corp. He was a ruthless strike-breaker and one of the nastiest industrialists of his day. Instead of receiving any comeuppance (though there were assassination attempts), he commissioned Carrère and Hastings to build him one of the last great Beaux Arts mansions on Fifth Avenue and filled it with his treasures. He bequeathed it to the nation as a memorial to himself.

The beautiful mansion on Fifth Avenue that usually houses the Frick collection will be closed for renovation and expansion

A new home Marcel Breuer created his five-story landmark building with spacious, airy galleries in 1966 for the Whitney Museum. It features a cantilevered facade surrounded by a moat-like space and bridge entrance. When the Whitney moved downtown, the Metropolitan Museum used the galleries temporarily for its modern collections. Now the spaces at the Breuer are adapted to showcase Frick's masterpieces. These include British (Constable, Gainsborough, Whistler, Turner), Dutch (Vermeer, Rembrandt, Van Eyck, Hals), Italian (Titian, Bellini, Veronese) and Spanish (El Greco, Goya, Velázquez) masters. Along with the paintings are enamel and porcelain, Persian carpets and Marie Antoinette's furniture. The new setting gives a fresh perspective on the collection.

THE BASICS

frick.org; frickfuture.org

➕ E7

✉ 945 Madison Avenue/ E 75th Street

☎ 212/288-0700

🕐 Check online

🚇 77th Street

🚌 M1, M2, M3, M4

♿ Good

💰 Expensive

❓ The anticipated renovation of the Frick is due to begin in 2020. Before visiting, check the website for updated information on offerings, hours and location of programming. Additional information about the project can be found at a separate website: frickfuture.org.

11 Grand Central Terminal

HIGHLIGHTS

- Main concourse ceiling
- Oyster Bar (▷ 148)
- Chandeliers
- Whispering Gallery
- The clock
- The 75ft (23m) arched windows
- Grand Staircase
- The Dining Concourse (▷ 145)
- Great Northern Food Hall

TIP

- After admiring the building, visit the many boutiques, gourmet market and annex of the New York Transit Museum.

Officially called Grand Central Terminal because the tracks all terminate here, this Beaux Arts masterpiece is not only an architectural marvel but also one of the biggest stations in the world.

Heart of the nation "Grand Central Station!" bellowed (erroneously) the 1937 opening of the eponymous NBC radio drama; "Beneath the glitter and swank of Park Avenue… Crossroads of a million private lives!…Heart of the nation's greatest city…" And so it is, and has been since 1871, when the first, undersize version of the station was opened by Commodore Cornelius Vanderbilt, who had bought up all the city's railroads. See him in bronze below Jules Alexis Coutan's allegorical statuary on the main facade (south, 42nd Street). The current

Clockwise from far left: The concourse of Grand Central Terminal; statuary by Jules Alexis Coutan on the main facade; Grand Central subway station; the Great Northern Food Hall; the four-faced clock; enjoy a platter of oysters in the famous Oyster Bar

building dates from 1913 and is another Beaux Arts glory, its design modeled partly on the Paris Opéra by the architectural firm Warren and Wetmore.

Look within Inside, the main concourse soars 12 stories high, with gleaming gold chandeliers and grand marble staircases at either end. Be careful what you say here—the acoustics are amazing. Look up at the ceiling for the stunning sight of 2,500 "stars" in an azure sky, with zodiac signs by French artist Paul Helleu. The fame of the brass clock with its four opalescent glass faces atop the information booth is out of proportion to its size. Below ground is a warren of 32 miles (52km) of tracks, tunnels and chambers; in one, the famed Oyster Bar (▷ 148) resides.

THE BASICS

grandcentralterminal.com

🚇 E11

✉ E 42nd Street/Park Avenue

☎ 212/340-2583

🕐 Daily 5.30am–2am

🍴 Restaurant, café/bar, snack bars

🚇 4, 5, 6, 7, S Grand Central–42nd Street

🚌 M1, M2, M3, M4, M42, M101, M102, M103 Grand Central

🚆 Metro North, Grand Central

♿ Good

💲 Free

❓ Both self-guided audio tours (moderate; daily 9–6) and the guided Municipal Art Society tours (expensive; daily 12.30pm) leave from the GCT Tour windows on the main concourse

HIGHLIGHTS

● Charming boutiques
● Washington Square Park
● NYC's narrowest house
(75½ Bedford Street)
● Christopher Park
● Halloween parade
● Jefferson Market Library
● Italian restaurants on
Bleecker Street
● MacDougal Street

TIP

● Free Tours by Foot is one
of several groups offering
guided tours; many self-
guided tours are also
available online.

The Village (never just "Greenwich") has
long been a bohemian magnet, and its
picturesque neighborhoods, lined with
trees and brownstones, form a romantic
image of Manhattan.

Artists, writers, musicians First settled by the
Dutch as Noortwijck, the Village became a
refuge in the 18th and early 19th centuries for
wealthy New Yorkers escaping epidemics in the
city. When the elite moved on, the bohemian
invasion began. Edgar Allan Poe moved to West
Third Street in 1845. Fellow literary habitués
included Mark Twain, O. Henry, Walt Whitman,
F. Scott Fitzgerald and Eugene O'Neill. After
World War II, artists Jackson Pollock, Mark
Rothko and Willem de Kooning also lived here.
Bob Dylan made his name in Village music

Clockwise from far left: Bars and restaurants abound in the Village; detail of the Gay Liberation Monument in Christopher Park; Bleecker Street has many restaurants; Christopher Street has great shops; getting around in the Village; desirable St. Luke's Place

clubs in the 1960s, while the Blue Note (▷ 132) and Village Vanguard clubs remain hotbeds of jazz today.

Freedom parades When police raided the Stonewall Inn on June 28, 1969, and arrested gay men for illegally buying drinks, they set off the Stonewall Riots—the birth of the Gay Rights movement. The Inn is on Christopher Street, which became the center of New York's gay community. Statues of gay and lesbian couples stand in tiny Christopher Park. The Washington Memorial Arch (▷ 73) towers over Washington Square Park, a lively hangout for university students. As you explore, look out for the ornate Jefferson Market Library (6th Avenue and W 10th Street), the quaint Cherry Lane Theatre on Commerce Street, and tiny Minetta Lane.

THE BASICS

➕ C17–D17

✉ East-west from Broadway to Hudson Street; north-south from 14th Street to Houston Street

🍴 Numerous

🚇 A, B, C, D, E, F 4th Street–Washington Square; 1 Christopher Street–Sheridan Square

🚌 M5

🚉 PATH Christopher Street

♿ Poor

HIGHLIGHTS

- The building
- *L'Hermitage à Pontoise*, Pissarro (1867)
- *Paris Through the Window*, Chagall (1913)
- *Woman Ironing*, Picasso (1904)
- *Nude*, Modigliani (1917)
- Kandinskys
- Klees
- Légers
- The store

TIP

- Museum admission is pay-what-you-wish on Saturdays 5–8, but get there early as lines can be long.

Now considered one of his masterpieces, Frank Lloyd Wright's spiral-shaped museum building was originally derided by critics, who compared it to a jello mold.

Museum of architecture This is the great architect's only major New York building. It was commissioned by Solomon R. Guggenheim at the urging of his friend and taste tutor Baroness Hilla von Rebay though, unfortunately, the wealthy metal-mining magnate died 10 years before it was completed in 1959. The giant white nautilus is certainly arresting, but it's the magnificent interior that captures the imagination the most. Take the elevator to the top level and snake your way down the museum's spiral ramp to experience the full effects of the building's design. You can study

Left: The spiral walkway inside the Guggenheim Museum; below: the Guggenheim's curvy exterior

the exhibits (albeit in reverse order), look over the parapet to the lobby below, and finish up where you began.

Museum of art There are some 6,000 pieces in the foundation's possession. Solomon and his wife Irene Rothschild abandoned collecting old masters when Hilla von Rebay introduced them to Léger, Kandinsky, Chagall, Mondrian, Moholy-Nagy and Gleizes, and they became hooked on the moderns. See early Picassos in the small rotunda and the tower extension. For Impressionists and Post-Impressionists, look for the Thannhauser Collection, always on display—unlike the rotated Guggenheim holdings, which are shown in themed exhibitions. The museum still acquires works, including pieces by Matthew Barney and Agathe Snow.

THE BASICS

guggenheim.org
⊞ E5
✉ 1071 5th Avenue/
89th Street
☎ 212/423-3500
🕐 Sun, Mon, Wed–Fri
10–5.30, Tue, Sat 10–8
🍴 Café
🚇 4, 5, 6 86th Street
🚌 M1, M2, M3, M4
♿ Good
💲 Expensive
❓ Pay-what-you-wish
entrance Sat 5–8

HIGHLIGHTS

- The Whitney Museum
- Site-specific art installations
- Northern spur preserve
- 10th Avenue Square
- High Line Plinth

TIP

- Because the park keeps entirely to the original rail line, narrow sections can be crowded. Come early before the day heats up or enjoy a leisurely stroll just before sunset.

Today, this beautiful elevated park attracts more annual visitors than the Statue of Liberty. Yet just a decade ago, the High Line was a weed-choked, abandoned rail line snaking through the industrial waterfront.

Train tracks Manhattan in the 19th century was the largest port in America, with many commercial piers lining the Hudson River. To move the huge amount of goods, Tenth Avenue was overlaid with railroad tracks so dangerous that the street was nicknamed Death Avenue. In the early 1930s, the trains were moved to a second-story elevated track running through many of the factories and warehouses, including the giant Nabisco headquarters (birthplace of the Oreo cookie) that is now Chelsea Market (▷ 120).

From left: View of New York's High Line Park, running under the Standard Hotel between 12th and 13th streets; planting on the High Line incorporates many hardy and perennial species that could once be found growing alongside the original rail tracks

Friends of the High Line After the freight line folded, the abandoned track became overgrown. In 1999, Friends of the High Line formed to advocate turning this wilderness into an amenity. A park now stretches 1.45 miles (2.3km) from Gansevoort Street to West 34th Street. Its popularity has transformed the neighborhood, drawing new luxury condos, hotels and restaurants. Where the tracks cross 10th Avenue at 17th Street, seating allows visitors to gaze uptown; a few steps south, an overgrown spur track recalls what the original High Line looked like. In summer, the park hosts temporary exhibitions, plus the High Line Plinth at the Spur, with contemporary art. The park's southern end joins the home of the Whitney Museum of American Art (▷ 60–61). The northern end borders Hudson Yards (▷ 68).

THE BASICS

thehighline.org
✚ A13, B13–16
✉ Gansevoort Street to W 34th Street between 10th and 12th avenues (staircases or elevators up to the park located every 2–3 blocks)
☎ 212/500-6035
🕐 Daily Jun–Sep 7am–11pm; Apr–May, Oct–Nov 7am–10pm; Dec–Mar 7–7
🍴 Seasonal
🚇 A, C, E 14th Street; L 8th Avenue; 7 34th Street–Hudson Yards
🚌 M11, M12, M14, M23, M34
💲 Free
♿ Good

HIGHLIGHTS

● Chandeliers in the Met foyer and auditorium
● Reflecting pool with Henry Moore's *Reclining Figure* (1965)
● Lincoln Center Out-of-Doors Festival in summer
● New York City Ballet's *Nutcracker* in December
● Chagall murals in the foyer of the Met
● Free concerts at the David Rubenstein Atrium
● New York Film Festival
● The Revson Fountain in the Central Plaza
● Jazz at Lincoln Center
● Annual *Messiah* singalong

TIP

● Dance under the stars at Midsummer Night's Swing, and enjoy summer events in the adjacent Damrosch Park.

Strolling across the Central Plaza to the fantastically lit 10-story colonnade of the Metropolitan Opera House on a deep winter's night is one of the most glamorous things you can do in this city, and you don't need tickets to come and look.

West Side Story The Rockefeller-funded arts center was envisaged in the late 1950s and finished in 1969, after 7,000 families and 800 businesses had been pushed aside by city planner Robert Moses. The opening scene of *West Side Story* was filmed here after the demolition began.

All the arts The 16-acre (6ha) site includes several of New York's top arts venues, all designed by different architects in the same

Clockwise from left: The Revson Fountain, between the David H. Koch Theater on the left and the Metropolitan Opera House on the right; the David Rubenstein Atrium is a great place to meet up with friends; aerial view of the Lincoln Center at night

white travertine. The Metropolitan Opera House is the glamor queen, with her vast Marc Chagall murals, red carpet, fabulous sweeping staircase and sparkling chandeliers that thrillingly rise to the gold-leaf ceiling before performances. You can take a fascinating backstage tour. David Geffen Hall is home to America's oldest orchestra, the NY Philharmonic, while the Juilliard School of Music supplies the ensemble with fresh talent. The David H. Koch Theater, housing the New York City Ballet, faces David Geffen Hall across the Plaza. The Frederick P. Rose Hall is the centerpiece of Jazz at Lincoln Center in the Time Warner Center down the street. Lincoln Center Theater, with three stages, the intimate Alice Tully Concert Hall and two movie theaters—Walter Reade and Elinor Bunin—complete the pack.

THE BASICS

lincolncenter.org

➕ B8

✉ 64th Street at Columbus Avenue

☎ Met Opera 212/362-6000, David Geffen Hall 212/875-5030, Jazz 212/258-9800, NYC Ballet 212/496-0600

🍴 Restaurants, cafés, bars

Ⓜ 1 66th Street–Lincoln Center

🚌 M5, M7, M10, M11, M66, M104

♿ Good

🎫 Center admission free

❓ Tours daily from David Rubenstein Atrium, tel 212/875-5350

43

HIGHLIGHTS

● Temple of Dendur (15BC)
● Period rooms, American Wing
● 19th- and early 20th-century art galleries
● Decorative arts from the Far East
● Greco-Roman galleries

TIP

● On Friday and Saturday evenings, when the museum stays open late, enjoy a cocktail and live music on the mezzanine.

The largest art museum in the western hemisphere has something for everyone, from ancient artifacts to arms and armor, cutting-edge fashion and some of the most famous paintings in the world.

Art history 101 The Met's collection is renowned for its stunning breadth and depth. The museum is so huge that visitors with limited time are well advised either to take a highlights tour with a museum guide or to choose one area to explore in depth, perhaps the European art galleries, the American Wing or the African carvings.

Two exceptional buildings Along with the Fifth Avenue location, the Met has another in Upper Manhattan: The Cloisters, a treasure of

Clockwise from left: The Met's European Sculpture Court; Wheat Field with Cypresses, Vincent van Gogh (1889), in the European Paintings and Sculpture Room; the Beaux Arts facade of the museum

European Medieval art and gardens (▷ 74). But the main building has ample treasures of its own to be discovered. These include the Egyptian Temple of Dendur, the Astor Court (a Ming Dynasty courtyard) in the Chinese galleries, a Frank Lloyd Wright living room in the American Wing, the dazzling changing exhibits of the Costume Institute and the Damascus Room in the Islamic collection. The 19-century galleries are home to works by Van Gogh, Degas and Monet.

Special exhibitions and more The museum fee includes special and traveling exhibitions as well as a changing summer installation. Many concerts, lectures and other events can be attended for an extra fee. Check the website in advance, as many of these sell out quickly.

THE BASICS

metmuseum.org

✚ D5–6

✉ 1000 5th Avenue/82nd Street

☎ 212/535-7710

🕐 Sun–Thu 10–5.30, Fri–Sat 10–9

🍴 Café, restaurant, bar

🚇 4, 5, 6 86th Street

🚌 M1, M2, M3, M4

♿ Good

💲 Expensive (includes Cloisters visit)

❓ Free guided tours leave from the lobby's info desk every 15 mins 10.15–4

HIGHLIGHTS

- *Hope*, Klimt (1907–08)
- *Dance*, Matisse (1909)
- *Les Demoiselles d'Avignon*, Picasso (1907)
- *Starry Night*, Van Gogh (1889)
- *Gas*, Hopper (1940)
- *One: Number 31*, Pollock (1950)
- *The Swimming Pool*, Matisse (1952)
- *An Orchid*, O'Keeffe (1941)
- *Self Portrait with Cropped Hair*, Kahlo (1940)

The latest major expansion of MoMA in 2019 added more than the vast new wing to showcase its famous collections. It brought a new approach to experiencing art and a broader world view, including more women and non-Western artists.

A pioneer from the start Since its founding in 1929, MoMA has been a leader in fostering appreciation of all the contemporary arts. The collections have grown to more than 200,000 pieces from paintings and sculptures to film, photography, architecture, industrial design, as well as video and sound innovations. The floors are set out in roughly chronological order but many galleries now display works in several mediums and styles. Where once photography and architecture were displayed separately,

From left: Gallery with Wilhelm Lehmbruck's Standing Youth to the fore and paintings by Chagall (left of the statue) and František Kupka (to the right); the stunning glass exterior of the MoMA, designed by the renowned Japanese architect Yoshio Taniguchi

rooms now move from one topic to another, filling your walk through the galleries with lovely surprises.

Art, art everywhere A map is essential for the stunning glass building that now occupies most of a city block. Free audio tours are also helpful. Favorites like Picasso, Matisse and Monet are on Floor 5, covering the 1880s to 1940s. Floor 4, the 1940s to 1970s, includes Warhol's *Gold Marilyn*, Matisse's cut-out room-size masterpiece, *The Swimming Pool*, and the Kravis Studio for acoustic art. Changing exhibits occupy Floor 3, while Floor 2 features work from the 1970s to today. Large assemblages fill the soaring atrium. Two main-floor galleries in the new west wing and the Sculpture Garden are free to the public.

THE BASICS

moma.org

➕ D10

✉ 11 W 53rd Street/ 5th–6th avenues

☎ 212/708-9400

🕐 Sat–Thu 10–5.30, Fri and first Thu of each month 10–9

🍴 Restaurant

Ⓔ E, M 5th Avenue–53rd Street; B, D, F 47th–50th streets–Rockefeller Center, 6, 51st Street

🚌 M1–M5, M7

♿ Good

💲 Expensive (includes special exhibitions and films); free Fri 5.30–9

HIGHLIGHTS

- Patience and Fortitude
- Rose Reading Room
- Thomas Jefferson's handwritten Declaration of Independence
- Astor Hall
- American Jewish Oral History Collection
- Gottesman Hall ceiling

TIP

- It's worth taking one of the free one-hour tours (Mon–Sat 11, 2; Sun 2). Meet at the reception desk in Astor Hall.

The New York Public Library's Central Research Building is a great, hushed palace, beautiful to behold even if you have no time to open any of its books. It is a US National Historic Landmark.

The building Along with the US Custom House (▷ 73) and Grand Central (▷ 34–35), this masterpiece by Carrère and Hastings is ranked as one of the best Beaux Arts buildings in New York and is a highlight of what was known as the City Beautiful era. In 2011, the library was rechristened the Stephen A. Schwarzman Building, after the Wall Street financier who donated $100 million toward its ongoing renovation. A pair of lions, named Patience and Fortitude by Mayor LaGuardia during the Depression, flank the stair that leads

Clockwise from far left: The Main Reading Room of the New York Public Library; Astor Hall, the starting point of guided tours; the exterior of the library, one of the finest Beaux Arts buildings in New York

into the white marble Astor Hall. Inside, see temporary exhibitions in the Gottesman Hall, and look skyward: the carved oak ceiling is sublime. Priceless items from the library's collection, such as the first Gutenberg Bible, line the balcony corridor or are displayed in upstairs rooms. Don't miss the stunning two-block-long reading rooms, or the Richard Haas murals of NYC publishing houses in the De Witt Wallace Periodical Room.

The books The library owns more than 18 million books, most of which are kept in the 92 branches. The 92 miles (148km) of holdings are solely for research. Books kept on the premises are sent to the reading room by dumbwaiter; for material kept offsite, researchers must make an appointment.

THE BASICS

nypl.org
✚ E12
✉ 476 5th Avenue/42nd Street
☎ 917/275-6975
🕙 Tue, Wed 10–7.45, Thu–Sat 10–5.45, Sun 1–4.45
🍴 Kiosks outside (summer)
🚇 4, 5, 6, S Grand Central–42nd Street; 7 5th Avenue
🚌 M1, M2, M3, M4, M5, M7, M42
🚆 Metro North, Grand Central
♿ Good
💲 Free

19 Rockefeller Center

HIGHLIGHTS

● Top of the Rock
Observation Deck
● 30 Rock's lobbies and the
Lee Lawrie friezes
● NBC studio tour
● Skating in winter
● Radio City Music Hall
● *Prometheus* (1934)
● *Atlas* (5th Avenue,
50th–51st streets)

TIP

● There's a vast array of
shops, casual restaurants
and more in a basement
arcade below the center.
There's a great vantage
point for watching winter
skaters down there, too.

This complex of art-deco buildings provides
many of those "this really is New York"
moments, especially at Christmas when you
can watch ice-skaters ringed by the flags of
the UN and gaze up at the massive tree.

Prometheus is here The 19-building
Rockefeller Center has been called the greatest
urban complex of the 20th century. John
D. Rockefeller Jr.'s grand real estate scheme
provided work for 40,000 people during the
Depression. Its centerpiece is the stepped
skyscraper at 30 Rockefeller Plaza (officially
now the Comcast Building, formerly the GE
Building), adorned with Lee Lawrie's glass-and-
limestone frieze, lobby murals by José Maria
Sert and various other artworks. Rest for a while
on a Channel Gardens bench and gaze on the

From far left: Radio City Music Hall forms part of Rockefeller Center; Paul Manship's bronze Prometheus (1934) *on the Lower Plaza; Friendship Between America and France (1934), a gilded bronze by Alfred Janniot above the Fifth Avenue entrance*

Lower Plaza, the ice rink and Paul Manship's gilded bronze *Prometheus* (1934).

Top of the Rock The three-tiered observation deck on the 70th floor of 30 Rock affords stunning panoramic views over Manhattan and the only public overview of Central Park. The mezzanine museum tells the history of the complex, before high-speed elevators whisk you to the 67th to 70th-floor viewing platforms.

NBC and Rockettes This is also the home of the NBC studios. Tours are led daily, or try for standby tickets to *Saturday Night Live* or one of the late-night talk shows filmed here. At Christmastime (and now in summer), the Rockettes hold court at Radio City Music Hall (▷ 136), the grandest theater in town.

THE BASICS

rockefellercenter.com
✚ D10–11, E10–11
✉ 5th–6th avenues/ 48th–51st streets
☎ 212/588-8601
🕐 Various
🍴 Many restaurants, cafés
🚇 B, D, F, M 47th–50th streets–Rockefeller Center
🚌 M1, M2, M3, M4, M5, M7, M50
♿ Moderate
🎟 Free
❓ Radio City tours, tel 866-858-0008; NBC Studio tours, tel 212/664-3700; Rockefeller Center tours, tel 212/698-2000

Top of the Rock
topoftherocknyc.com
☎ 212/698-2000
🕐 Daily 8am–12.30am (last elevator 11.55pm)
💵 Expensive

HIGHLIGHTS

- Shopping
- King and Queen of Greene Street
- Little Singer Building
- Haughwout Building

TIP

- A lively French bistro serving breakfast, lunch and dinner, Balthazar (80 Spring Street/Crosby Street) has been a SoHo favorite since 1997.

In the last 150 years, SoHo has come full circle. New York's smartest shopping district around the time of the Civil War, the area fell on hard times by World War II. Now, its landmark cast-iron buildings teem with fashionable shops again.

Cast in iron An acronym for "South of Houston," SoHo stretches for several delightful blocks between Houston and Canal streets, bordered by Lafayette Street on the east and Sixth Avenue to the west. Around 500 of its 19th-century industrial buildings have been preserved in the SoHo Cast Iron Historic District. Inexpensive, strong and easy to mold, cast iron made it possible to erect ornate buildings in Italianate and other elaborate styles quickly and cheaply. Some of the finest examples

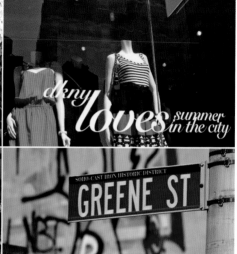

Clockwise from far left: The Little Singer Building in the SoHo Cast Iron Historic District; sculpture inspired by the well-known 1932 photograph of New York ironworkers eating lunch while sitting on a girder; fashion stores; Greene Street is a great place to stroll; art galleries abound

are the King (No. 72) and Queen (No. 28) of Greene Street, the Little Singer Building (561 Broadway) and the Haughwout Building (488 Broadway), which had the first Otis steam passenger elevator. Old-fashioned lampposts further enhance SoHo's charm.

Art and fashion By the 1960s and 1970s, many of SoHo's commercial buildings were abandoned. Then, artists moved in, art galleries followed, and SoHo became the most fashionable quarter in town. Rising prices forced many artists and galleries to Chelsea and beyond, but fashionistas quickly filled the empty and spacious showrooms. Everything from Prada's flagship store to branches of Bloomingdale's and Britain's Topshop, along with designer boutiques, make this a shopper's heaven.

THE BASICS

- E18–19
- Houston–Canal streets, Lafayette Street– 6th Avenue
- Numerous
- R, W Prince Street; C, E, 6 Spring Street
- M5, M21
- Moderate

HIGHLIGHTS

● View from the crown
● Statue of Liberty Museum, including the original torch
● Fort Wood, the star-shaped pedestal base

TIP

● Visits to the crown must be reserved well in advance (sometimes 3–4 months) on tel 201/604-2800 or online at statuecruises.com. There are no same-day crown tickets available.

Liberty Enlightening the World (as she's formally known), famous symbol of the American dream of freedom, takes your breath away, however many times you've seen her image.

How she grew In the late 1860s, sculptor Frédéric-Auguste Bartholdi dreamed of placing a monument to freedom in a prominent location. His dream merged with the French historian Edouard-René de Laboulaye's idea of presenting the American people with a statue that celebrated freedom and the two nations' friendship. Part of the idea was to shame the repressive French government but, apparently, New Yorkers took their freedom for granted. It was only after Joseph Pulitzer promised to print the name of every donor in his newspaper, the

From left: Liberty Island, a beacon of hope since 1886; Liberty's seven-pointed crown; the symbol of American liberty raises her torch to the world

New York World, that citizens coughed up the funds to build the pedestal. Liberty was unveiled by President Grover Cleveland on October 28, 1886.

Mother of exiles Beneath her 25ft-long (8m) feet, she tramples the shackles of tyranny, and her seven-pointed crown beams liberty to the seven continents and the seven seas. Gustave Eiffel designed the 1,700-bar iron and steel supporting structure. She weighs 225 tons, is 151ft (46m) tall, and is covered in 300 copper plates. The tablet she holds reads: July IV MDCCLXXVI—the date of the Declaration of Independence. The torch tip towers 305ft (93m) above sea level. In the museum in the statue's base you can read Emma Lazarus's stirring poem, *The New Colossus*.

THE BASICS

nps.gov/stli
🔁 See map ▷ 110
✉ Liberty Island
☎ 212/363-3200
🕐 Daily 8.30–5 (last ferry departs 3.30); extended hours in peak season. A limited number of daily tickets to tour the pedestal/ museum may be reserved in advance from the ferry office, by phone or online
🍴 Café
🚇 4, 5 Bowling Green, 1 South Ferry, then take ferry
🚌 M5, M15, M20 South Ferry, then take ferry
⛴ Departs Battery Park
☎ 877/523-9849; statuecruises.com
♿ Poor
💲 Free; ferry expensive

HIGHLIGHTS

● Neon lights at night
● Broadway Plaza
● 42nd Street
● ABC's *Good Morning* studio: 44th/Broadway
● New Year's Eve ball drop

TIP

● The TKTS booth at Duffy Square, 47th Street/ Broadway, discounts same-day theater tickets and is open daily 3–8 for evening shows, Wed, Thu and Sat 10–2 for matinees, Sun 11–3 for matinees, 3–7 for evening shows. Other locations: Lincoln Center and South Street Seaport.

"The Crossroads of the World," one-time symbol of Manhattan glitz and glamor, is bright, bold and exciting—there is always something going on here. Beneath the dazzling neon signs, big-name stores and entertainment venues do a brisk trade.

Longacre Square The junction of Broadway and Seventh Avenue was called Longacre Square until the Times Tower, the new home of the *New York Times*, was finished in 1904. Almost immediately, the relocation of the theater district, the opening of the first subway and the decision to site the New Year celebration here made it the symbolic center of Manhattan.

On Broadway The theaters moved into the area, and Broadway, the Great White Way,

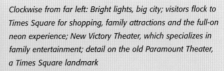

Clockwise from far left: Bright lights, big city; visitors flock to Times Square for shopping, family attractions and the full-on neon experience; New Victory Theater, which specializes in family entertainment; detail on the old Paramount Theater, a Times Square landmark

became synonymous with big-time showbiz with its popular shows, particularly musicals. By 1914 there were some 43 theaters in the immediate vicinity of the square; after multiple closures, refurbishments and reopenings, there are 41 of them today.

Best of Times, worst of Times By the 1970s Times Square was decaying, many of the legitimate theaters having fallen on hard times and become porn theaters. But a massive clean-up effort in the 1990s brought about the area's rebirth. Today it's a tourist hot spot, with a raft of family attractions, megastores and restaurants beneath the glittering state-of-the-art illuminations. A large section of Times Square is now traffic-free, though the human traffic jams are bigger than ever.

THE BASICS

timessquarenyc.org

✚ D11

🚇 1, 2, 3, 7, N, Q, R, S Times Square–42nd Street

🚌 M5, M7, M20, M42, M104

❓ Visit the Tourist Information kiosk in Broadway Plaza for up-to-date happenings in and around the square

TKTS Booth: tdf.org/nyc/81/TKTS-Live provides real-time updates of what is on offer before you commit to standing in line

HIGHLIGHTS

● Trinity Church
● Federal Hall
● New York Stock
Exchange
● The House of Morgan

TIP

● Weekend mornings are
quietest in this part of
town. To experience the
hustle and bustle of Wall
Street traders, come
Mon–Fri around lunch.

Depending on your point of view, Wall
Street is the blessing or blight of the world's
economic fortunes. But either way, the
historic buildings and urban buzz of this
financial powerhouse are fascinating to see
and experience.

The Buttonwood Agreement Wall Street,
named for the Dutch colonial wall that once
marked the city's northern boundary, is the
epicenter of the financial district. It has been so
since the late 18th century, when businessmen
gathered here under a buttonwood tree to
trade bonds, issued to finance debts incurred in
the Revolutionary War. In 1792, 24 traders
signed the Buttonwood Agreement, which
created the New York Stock Exchange. Today,
the NYSE is the largest stock exchange in the

Clockwise from far left: The New York Stock Exchange; the soaring towers of Wall Street; Federal Hall, fronted by a bronze statue of George Washington and modeled on the Greek Parthenon; the beautifully decorated domed ceiling in the entrance of Federal Hall

world. The 1903 building, with its grand trading floor and facade of Corinthian columns, stands at the corner with Broad Street.

A million-dollar stroll At the west end of Wall Street stands Trinity Church (1846), the third on this site. The original, built in 1699, was the city's first church. Alexander Hamilton and other famous New Yorkers are buried in the church-yard. At the corner of Wall and Broad streets sits the House of Morgan, formerly owned by J.P. Morgan & Co, and once the most powerful financial institution in America (now housing apartments). On April 30, 1789, George Washington was sworn in as America's first president at Federal Hall, now a national memorial and museum. 40 Wall Street is also known as the Trump Building.

THE BASICS

downtownny.com
nps.gov/feha
moaf.org
trinitywallstreet.org

✚ E22

✉ NYSE, 18 Broad Street; Federal Hall, 26 Wall Street; Trinity Church, Broadway at Wall Street

☎ Federal Hall 212/825-6990; Trinity Church 212/602-0800

🕐 Federal Hall Mon–Fri 9–5; Trinity Church daily 7–6

🍴 Restaurants, pubs

🚇 2, 3, 4, 5 Wall Street; J, Z Broad Street

🚌 M5

♿ Federal Hall free; Trinity Church free

❓ Tours: Download Trinity Church's guided tour app from its website

Gertrude Vanderbilt Whitney's world-class collection, a showcase of her work and that of her friends, was first shown in a modest Greenwich Village studio space in 1918. Today, the collection is housed in the stunning and innovative Renzo Piano-designed headquarters along the High Line.

No room at the Met Sculptor and patron of her contemporaries' work, Gertrude Vanderbilt Whitney offered her collection of 700 modern artworks to the Met in 1929, but the great institution turned up its nose. Whitney instead formalized her own museum space, first in the Village, and then on the Upper East Side. Renzo Piano's Meatpacking District building has greatly expanded the museum's footprint, allowing more room for shows. The Whitney's collection

From left: The museum's new home is a 21st-century architectural gem; the Whitney hosts a biennial exhibition of contemporary art

WHITNEY BIENNIAL

reads like a roll call of American 20th-century greats: Edward Hopper, Thomas Hart Benton, Willem de Kooning, Georgia O'Keeffe, Claes Oldenburg, Jasper Johns, George Bellows and Jackson Pollock are perhaps the best known.

Take your pick Exhibitions, drawn from the museum's permanent collection, often emphasize a single artist's work. At other times, they prove more eclectic. The Whitney Biennial (in the spring of even-numbered years) presents the curator's vision—sometimes controversial—of the leading trends in American art during the past two years and often features the work of lesser-known artists. The famous showcase has boosted the careers of artists such as Edward Hopper (who appeared in the first exhibition in 1932), Sheila Hicks and Jenny Holzer.

THE BASICS

whitney.org
➕ B16
✉ 99 Gansevoort Street/ Washington Street
☎ 212/570-3600
🕐 Sun–Mon, Wed–Thu 10.30–6, Fri–Sat 10.30–10
🍴 Restaurant, café
🚇 A, C, E 14th Street; L 8th Avenue
🚌 M14
♿ Good
💲 Expensive (under 18s free); donation Fri 7–10
❓ Free daily tours

From the ashes of the World Trade Center
that was destroyed by terrorists in 2001,
a vibrant contemporary center has emerged,
transforming the neighborhood while
still honoring the memory of that tragic
event. Five new buildings have replaced
the original two. One World Trade Center,
known as the Freedom Tower, remains the
city's tallest.

**The National September 11 Memorial and
Museum** Architects Michael Arad and Peter
Walker won an international contest for their
memorial design entitled *Reflecting Absence*.
It comprises two square waterfalls, situated
over the footprint of the towers. The waterfalls
cascade 30ft (9m) into pools that disappear
into a central void. Bronze panels are inscribed

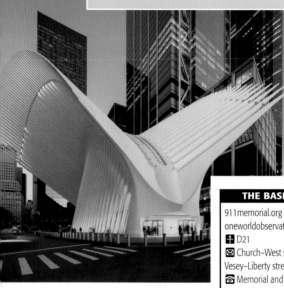

Clockwise from far left: The Oculus mezzanine, designed by Santiago Calatrava; waterfalls at the National September 11 Memorial; the National September 11 Memorial at Ground Zero; One World Observatory

with the names of almost 3,000 known victims. A memorial park with more than 300 oak trees offers a peaceful space for contemplation. The underground museum provides a history of the site. New constructions like Santiago Calatrava's futuristic Oculus, a transportation hub and shopping center, have enlivened the area and the revived World Financial Center nearby, now known as Brookfield Place (▷ 66), has added more shopping and waterfront dining.

One World Observatory At the top of One World Trade Center is One World Observatory, with 360-degree views of Manhattan, Brooklyn, New York Harbor and beyond. "Sky Pods" (or elevators) with stunning animations of Manhattan's 400-year development whisk visitors up 100 stories in 60 seconds.

THE BASICS

911memorial.org
oneworldobservatory.com

🚇 D21

✉ Church–West streets, Vesey–Liberty streets

☎ Memorial and museum: 212/266-5211; observatory: 844/696-1776

🕐 Memorial: daily 7.30am–9pm; museum: Sun–Thu 9–8 (last entry at 6), Fri–Sat 9–9 (last entry at 7); observatory: daily, check times online

🚇 E World Trade Center; 2, 3, 4, 5, A, C, J, Z Fulton Street

🚌 M5, M20, M22

♿ Good

🎫 Memorial free; museum and observatory expensive; limited free museum tickets Tue after 4pm

More to See

This section contains other great places to visit if you have more time. Some are in the heart of the city while others are a short journey away, found under Farther Afield.

In the Heart of the City

AMERICAN FOLK ART MUSEUM

folkartmuseum.org

Excellent changing exhibits of folk art from around the world make this small museum well worth a visit. Examples of the vast permanent collection of quilts, paintings and crafts are also on display, dating from the 18th century to today. The shop has a superb range of hand-crafted items.

🔁 C8 ✉ 2 Lincoln Square (Columbus Avenue between 65th and 66th streets) ☎ 212/595-9533 🕐 Tue–Thu, Sat 11.30–7, Fri 12–7.30, Sun 12–6 🚇 1 66th Street–Lincoln Center 🎫 Free

BATTERY PARK

thebattery.org

At the southernmost tip of Manhattan, with splendid views of New York Harbor, Battery Park was named for the cannon sited here to defend the fledgling city against British attack. Ferries to the Statue of Liberty and Ellis Island leave from Castle Clinton National Monument, a former fort. Among the many monuments in the park,

look for *The Immigrants* sculpture (near Castle Clinton), a symbol of New York's enduring role as a city of emigrés.

🔁 E23 ✉ Tip of Manhattan 🚇 1 South Ferry; 4, 5 Bowling Green

BROOKFIELD PLACE

bfplny.com

The former World Financial Center has been refurbished with many shopping and dining options and regular free entertainment in the soaring central Winter Garden. Dine outdoors for views of the yacht basin and the Statue of Liberty beyond.

🔁 D21 ✉ 230 Vesey Street/West Street ☎ 212/978-1673 🕐 Mon–Sat 10–9, Sun 12–6, dining one hour later 🍴 Restaurants, cafés 🚇 World Trade Center, 2, 3 Park Place; A, C Chambers Street

BROOKLYN BRIDGE

Completed in 1883, the Brooklyn Bridge was the first to link Manhattan and Brooklyn. With its twin Gothic towers and graceful ballet of cables, it is one of New York's finest landmarks. Stroll

The American Folk Art Museum

Brooklyn Bridge

across the pedestrian walkway for views of the Manhattan skyline.
⊞ G21 🚇 4, 5, 6 Brooklyn Bridge–City Hall

CHELSEA GALLERY DISTRICT

When real-estate prices in SoHo began to skyrocket in the 1990s, the downtown galleries moved to Chelsea. Today, there are over 100 galleries in the neighborhood, primarily located between 10th and 11th avenues. As most galleries are closed on both Sunday and Monday, art lovers should plan accordingly. Gallery hopping, you can take in everything from established artists to Modernist masters to stars of the up-and-coming generation.
⊞ B14 ✉ From 27th Street south to 19th Street, and 9th Avenue west to the Hudson River 🚇 1, 18th, 23rd, 28th streets–7th Avenue; C, E, 23rd streets–8th Avenue

CHRYSLER BUILDING

The gleaming art-deco spire of the Chrysler Building is an iconic symbol of New York. When

The Chrysler Building

completed in 1931, it held the title of "world's tallest building" until it was surpassed by the Empire State Building the same year. Every detail of the 77-story building evokes a 1929 Chrysler Plymouth. The winged steel gargoyles are modeled on its radiator caps; the building's stepped setbacks carry stylized hubcaps and the spire resembles a radiator grille. You can visit the lobby to see the art-deco detailing in the red marble, granite and chrome interior, surmounted by the 97ft by 100ft (30m by 31m) mural depicting industrial scenes and celebrating "transportation." Don't miss the art-deco marquetry on the elevator doors.
⊞ F11 ✉ 405 Lexington Avenue/42nd Street 🕙 Mon–Fri office hours 🚇 4, 5, 6, 7, S Grand Central–42nd Street 🚌 M42, M101, M102, M103 🚆 Metro North, Grand Central ♿ Good 💲 Free

CITY HALL

nyc.gov/html/artcom
Built between 1803 and 1812 in Federal and French Renaissance styles, this is one of the nation's oldest city halls. The building and the rotunda, with its cantilevered marble staircase, Corinthian columns and coffered dome, are designated landmarks. See the Governor's Room furniture and portrait collection, consisting of more than 100 paintings, on a guided tour.
⊞ E21 ✉ Broadway/Murray Street ☎ 311 or 212/788-2656 🕙 Wed noon (register on the day 10–11.30 at the NYC Tourism Kiosk at the southern end of City Hall Park, east side of Broadway at Barclay Street) and Thu 10 (online reservations required) 🚇 2, 3 Park Place; 4, 5, 6 Brooklyn Bridge–City Hall; R City Hall 💲 Free

ELDRIDGE STREET SYNAGOGUE

eldridgestreet.org

Built in 1887, this synagogue is a symbol of the aspirations of Eastern European immigrants on the Lower East Side. Its 50ft (15m) vaulted ceiling, Moorish and Romanesque details and stained-glass windows make it one of the city's architectural gems. Exhibits and guided tours point out design features and tell the story of this diverse neighborhood.
➕ G19 ✉ 12 Eldridge Street ☎ 212/219-0302 🕓 Sun–Thu 10–5, Fri 10–3 🚇 F East Broadway; B, D Grand Street 🚹 Good 🎟 Moderate

FLATIRON BUILDING

This 1902 skyscraper, designed by Daniel Burnham, was named for its amazing and memorable shape. It is an isosceles triangle with a sharp angle pointing uptown. This shape has made it one of the most recognizable buildings in the city.
➕ E14 ✉ 175 5th Avenue/E 22nd–23rd streets 🚇 N, R 23rd Street

GULLIVER'S GATE

gulliversgate.com

From the Great Wall of China to the Egyptian pyramids to New York City, wonders of the world in miniature await at this attraction near Times Square, in a lavish display covering 50,000sq ft (4,645sq m).
➕ D11 ✉ 216 W 44th Street ☎ 212/235-2016 🕓 Daily 10–8 🚇 1, 2, 3, 7, N, Q, R, S Times Square 🎟 Expensive

HUDSON YARDS

hudsonyardsnewyork.com

A mini-city built on platforms above working rail yards has emerged on 28 acres (11.33h) of Manhattan's far west side. Office and apartment towers surround The Shed, a venue for cutting-edge entertainment, and a shiny seven-story shopping–dining mall with the city's first Neiman Marcus department store. In the midst of it all is Vessel, Thomas Heatherwick's whimsical 16-story climbing maze. Due in 2020 is the Edge, a triangular wedge reaching 65ft (20m) into the blue that will be the city's highest outdoor viewing point.

The Jewish Museum chronicles the history of Jewish communities worldwide

There is ample landscaped open space to take it all in.

🚇 B13 ✉ 10th to12th Avenues, West 30th to West 34th Streets ☎ 646/954-3100; The Shed 646/455-3494 🕐 Mon–Sat 10–9, Sun 11–7 🍴 Restaurants, cafés 🚇 7 Hudson Yards

JEWISH MUSEUM

thejewishmuseum.org

The largest Jewish museum in the western hemisphere chronicles Jewish experiences worldwide. Artifacts in the permanent collection cover 4,000 years of Jewish history, while special exhibitions focus on Jewish art and culture.

🚇 E4 ✉ 1109 5th Avenue/92nd Street ☎ 212/423-3200 🕐 Fri–Tue 11–5.45, Thu 11–8 🍴 Café 🚇 4, 5, 6 86th Street 💵 Expensive; free Sat

MORGAN LIBRARY & MUSEUM

themorgan.org

This collection of literary works, rare musical manuscripts and artworks was amassed by financier J.P. Morgan, whose palatial library alone is worth the visit. Highlights include a copy of the Gutenberg Bible, music scores by Beethoven, Mozart and Puccini, etchings by Raphael and Michelangelo and manuscripts by Dickens and Twain.

🚇 E12 ✉ 225 Madison Avenue/E 36th Street ☎ 212/685-0008 🕐 Tue–Thu 10.30–5, Fri 10.30–9, Sat 10–6, Sun 11–6 🚇 6 33rd Street; 4, 5, 6, 7 Grand Central 💵 Expensive

EL MUSEO DEL BARRIO

elmuseo.org

This museum dedicated to Latin American and Caribbean art contains over 8,000 items, from pre-Columbian artifacts to modern paintings and photographs.

🚇 E2 ✉ 1230 5th Avenue/104th Street ☎ 212/831-7272 🕐 Wed–Sat 11–6, Sun 12–5 🚇 6 103rd Street 💵 Moderate

MUSEUM OF ARTS AND DESIGN

madmuseum.org

MAD showcases crafts, art and design through an impressive collection, special exhibitions and public programs, while the monthly Studio Sundays allow families to join creative activities.

Museum of Arts and Design

C9 ✉ 2 Columbus Circle ☎ 212/299-2777 🕐 Tue, Wed, Fri–Sun 10–6, Thu 10–9 🍴 Restaurant 🚇 1, A, B, C, D 59th Street–Columbus Circle 🎟 Moderate (by donation Thu 6–9pm)

MUSEUM OF CHINESE IN AMERICA

mocanyc.org

The permanent collection tells the story of Chinese immigration across the USA. Temporary exhibits examine aspects of the contemporary Chinese-American experience.

F19 ✉ 215 Centre Street/Grand Street ☎ 212/619-4785 🕐 Tue–Wed, Fri–Sun 11–6, Thu 11–9 🚇 6, J, N, Q, R, Z Canal Street 🎟 Moderate

MUSEUM OF THE CITY OF NEW YORK

mcny.org

Changing exhibits bring to life the city's past and present. Collections include photos, toys, furniture and decorative arts. There's also a light installation in the Rotunda.

E2 ✉ 1220 5th Avenue/103rd Street ☎ 212/534-1672 🕐 Daily 10–6 🚇 6 103rd Street 🎟 Expensive

Neue Galerie

NATIONAL GEOGRAPHIC ENCOUNTER: OCEAN ODYSSEY

natgeoencounter.com

This virtual-reality experience near Times Square uses technology to take visitors on an underwater journey across the Pacific Ocean to see stunning sea creatures, including sea lions, whales and sharks. You'll also hear stories from National Geographic explorers.

D11 ✉ 226 West 44th Street/7th and 8th avenues ☎ 646/308-1337 🕐 Sun–Thu 10–9, Fri–Sat 9am–10pm 🚇 Times Square 🎟 Expensive

NEUE GALERIE

neuegalerie.org

Dedicated to early 20th-century German and Austrian art and design, the highlight is Gustav Klimt's portrait *Adele Bloch-Bauer I* (1907), known as "The Lady in Gold." European decorative arts and the Bauhaus are also represented, with contributions from the likes of Marcel Breuer and Walter Gropius.

E5 ✉ 1048 5th Avenue/86th Street ☎ 212/994-9493 🕐 Thu–Mon 11–6 🍴 Café 🚇 4, 5, 6 86th Street 🎟 Expensive

NEW MUSEUM

newmuseum.org

The dynamic building resembling giant white boxes stacked askew is a fitting home for this cutting-edge museum of contemporary art. The seventh-floor balcony affords panoramic views.

F18 ✉ 235 Bowery/Prince Street ☎ 212/219-1222 🕐 Tue–Wed, Fri–Sun 11–6, Thu 11–9 (Thu 7–9 pay what you wish) 🍴 Café 🚇 N, R Prince Street 🎟 Expensive ❓ Free tours at 12.30, and at 3 on Thu, Sat and Sun

NEW-YORK HISTORICAL SOCIETY

nyhistory.org

With 1.5 million objects from the Colonial era to today, the society uses immersive films and changing exhibits to traces the growth of New York from Dutch trading post to today's powerful city. Recent additions include the Center for Women's History and a children's museum downstairs. Eclectic exhibits include fragments from America's first capitol building, shackles worn by a child slave, noted collections of Audubon bird prints and Tiffany lamps.

✚ C6 ✉ Central Park West/77th Street ☎ 212/873-3400 🕐 Tue–Thu and Sat 10–6, Fri 10–8, Sun 11–5 🚇 B, C 81st Street 💲 Expensive

RUBIN MUSEUM OF ART

rubinmuseum.org

A superb collection of art from the Himalayan region. It comprises religious art and cultural artifacts, including scroll paintings, sculptures, ritual objects, textiles and prints. There is also a rich program of cultural events, such as music, meditation and movies.

✚ D15 ✉ 150 W 17th Street/7th Avenue ☎ 212/620-5000 🕐 Mon, Thu 11–5, Wed 11–9, Fri 11–10, Sat–Sun 11–6 🍴 Café 🚇 1 18th Street–7th Avenue 💲 Expensive, free Fri 6–10 ❓ Free tours 1pm and 3pm

ST. PATRICK'S CATHEDRAL

saintpatrickscathedral.org

With its ornate spires soaring 330ft (100m) above Fifth Avenue, James Renwick's cathedral, built in 1858–79, seats 2,200 people. The St. Michael and St. Louis altar was designed by Tiffany & Co., while the rose window is one of stained-glass artist Charles J. Connick's finest creations. Thanks to a recent major $200 million restoration, the outside stone work and massive doors have new polish and the ceiling that had darkened is once again aglow.

✚ E10 ✉ 5th Avenue between E 50th and E 51st streets ☎ 212/753-2261 🕐 Daily 6.30am–8.45pm; services at various times 🚇 6 51st Street; E, M 5th Avenue–53rd Street 💲 Free ❓ Guided tours available (expensive)

The dynamic New Museum

The Rubin Museum of Art

ST. PATRICK'S OLD CATHEDRAL

oldcathedral.org

New York's first Roman Catholic cathedral opened in 1815, when the area was settled by Irish immigrants. The building has a stunning hand-carved altarpiece filled with statuary. The small graveyard is a place for contemplation.

🔡 F18 ⊠ Mott Street between Prince and Houston streets ☎ 212/226-8075 (call for times) ⏰ Sat–Sun, hours may vary 🚇 N, R, Prince Street 💷 Free

ST. PAUL'S CHAPEL

trinitywallstreet.org

George Washington worshiped here in the city's only remaining Colonial church. The fine 1766 Georgian interior and chandeliers sparkle after recent restoration. Spared damage on 9/11, this became an area of refuge. The Bell of Liberty in the churchyard, a gift from a London church, tolls to mark the anniversary each year.

🔡 E21 ⊠ 209 Broadway at Fulton Street ☎ 212/602-0800 ⏰ Daily 10–6 🚇 2, 3, 4, 5, A, C, J, Z Fulton Street 💷 Free

Spyscape

SOUTH STREET SEAPORT

southstreetseaport.com

Relive the city's maritime history and enjoy waterfront dining at this cobble-stoned historic district. Museum admission includes boarding vintage ships, and boat trips are offered in summer. Pier 17, the dining center, now has a number of celebrity chefs. There are shops galore, plus 19th-century printing demostrations at Bowne Stationers.

🔡 G21 ⊠ Fulton Street at Water Street ☎ Museum 212/748-8600 ⏰ Museum: Wed–Sun 11–5 🚇 2, 3, 4, 5, A, C, J, Z Fulton Street 💷 Expensive

SPYSCAPE

spyscape.com

This high-tech challenge is all about testing visitors' ability as spies, with kiosks that measure intelligence, personality and risk-taking potential. Exhibits chronicle spy landmarks like the Enigma code machine.

🔡 C10 ⊠ 928 8th Avenue/55th Street ☎ 212/549-1941 ⏰ Mon–Thu 10–9, Fri 10–10, Sat–Sun 9–9 🚇 C, E 50th Street; N, Q, R, W 57th Street 💷 Expensive

TENEMENT MUSEUM

tenement.org

This reconstruction of life in an 1863 tenement block is a must for history buffs. Guided tours of the apartments focus on the homes and workshops of Jewish, Italian, Irish and later Puerto Rican and Polish immigrants who lived here. There are also walking tours of the neighborhood.

🔡 G18 ⊠ 103 Orchard Street ☎ 877-975-3786 ⏰ Tours daily 10–5.45, 🚇 F, J, M, Z Delancey Street–Essex Street; B, D Grand Street 💷 Expensive

UNION SQUARE

Named for the union of Broadway and Fourth Avenue, this is where downtown and uptown meet. It is ringed with restaurants and shops and, four days a week, has the city's best and biggest market, selling homegrown produce (▷ 125)—it's a great option for a picnic lunch. This is also the site of one of the city's largest and most colorful December holiday bazaars, filled with booths stocked with original gifts.

🚪 E15 ⊠ E 14th–17th streets, Park Avenue South, Broadway 🍴 Greenmarket Mon, Wed, Fri, Sat 8–6 🍴 Numerous 🚇 4, 5, 6, L, N, Q, R 14th Street–Union Square 🚌 M3 ♿ Good

UNITED NATIONS HEADQUARTERS

visit.un.org

Take a guided tour to see the General Assembly Hall and collection of art and artifacts donated from around the world. A limited number of same-day tickets are available on site, but it's much better to buy them online in advance. Arrive at least one hour early for security screening.

🚪 G11 ⊠ 1st Avenue/45th–46th streets ☎ 212/963-8687 🕐 Mon–Fri 9–4.45 (a guided tour ticket is required) 🍴 Café, restaurant 🚇 4, 5, 6, 7 to Grand Central 💷 Expensive ❓ The Visitor Center (open daily) is worth a stop; its shop features products from all over the world. Also check out Rodney Leon's "The Ark of Return," a memorial to the victims of the slave trade

US CUSTOM HOUSE

nmai.si.edu/visit/newyork

Also known as the Alexander Hamilton US Custom House, this 1907 Beaux Arts beauty, designed by Cass Gilbert, now houses the Smithsonian's National Museum of the American Indian, highlighting native cultures of North, Central and South America. The expansive permanent collection includes items ranging from ancient Paleo-Indian cultures to contemporary arts; there are also excellent changing exhibitions.

🚪 E23 ⊠ 1 Bowling Green ☎ 212/514-3700 🕐 Fri–Wed 10–5, Thu 10–8 🚇 4, 5 Bowling Green; 1 South Ferry 💷 Free

WASHINGTON SQUARE

nycgovparks.org/parks/washington-square-park

The square is a prime people-watching spot in the Village. At the north end, Washington Memorial Arch, designed by Stanford White, marks the start of Fifth Avenue. Notice "The Row" of Greek Revival homes (Nos. 1–13) where the elite of 19th-century New York lived. If you want to get a real feel for the place, read Henry James's *Washington Square* first.

🚪 E17 🚇 R, W 8th Street–NYU; A, B, C, D, E, F, M 4th Street–Washington Square

The US Custom House

Farther Afield

BRONX ZOO

bronxzoo.com

The biggest city zoo in the US has more than 4,000 animals and is a leader in wildlife conservation. Don't miss the Congo Gorilla Forest, or the Wild Asia Complex with its monorail. There is also a new zipline that glides 45ft (13.7m) above the Bronx River.

See map ▷ 111 Fordham Road (Bronx River Parkway Northeast) 718/220-5100 Apr–Oct Mon–Fri 10–5, Sat–Sun 10–5.30; Nov–Mar daily 10–4.30 Restaurant, café 2 Pelham Parkway Expensive (Wed discounts)

THE CLOISTERS

metmuseum.org/visit/visit-the-cloisters

This castle on a hilltop, filled with treasures, is the medieval branch of the Met. It is known for its exquisite tapestries, stained-glass windows, statuary, a Gothic chapel and serene gardens. John D. Rockerfeller Jr. was largely responsible for the building and its holdings. Also included is the rare collection amassed by sculptor George Grey Barnard.

See map ▷ 111 Fort Tryon Park, North Manhattan 212/923-3700 Mar–Oct daily 10–5.15; Nov–Feb 10–4.45 A 190th Street Expensive (Met Museum admission includes entry to The Cloisters)

CONEY ISLAND

coneyisland.com

At the end of the 19th century, on a peak day Coney Island played host to a million people. Since then, attractions have come and gone but the big dipper ride, the Cyclone, is still here and Nathan's Famous hot dogs are still sold from the original site. MCU Park, home of the Brooklyn Cyclones baseball team, also hosts concerts. New amusement parks are revitalizing the area and the Aquarium has a spectacular shark exhibit.

See map ▷ 110 Surf Avenue, Boardwalk; Aquarium: W 8th Street, Surf Avenue Aquarium 718/265-3474 Jun–early Sep daily 10–5; Sep–Oct, Apr–May Mon–Fri 10–4, Sat–Sun 10–4.30; Nov–Mar daily 10–3.30 Cafés D, F, N, Q Coney Island–Stillwell Avenue Aquarium moderate, rides expensive

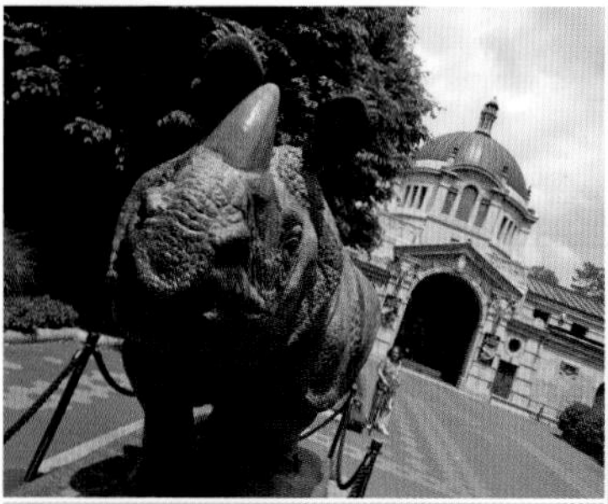

Bronx Zoo, the largest city zoo in the US

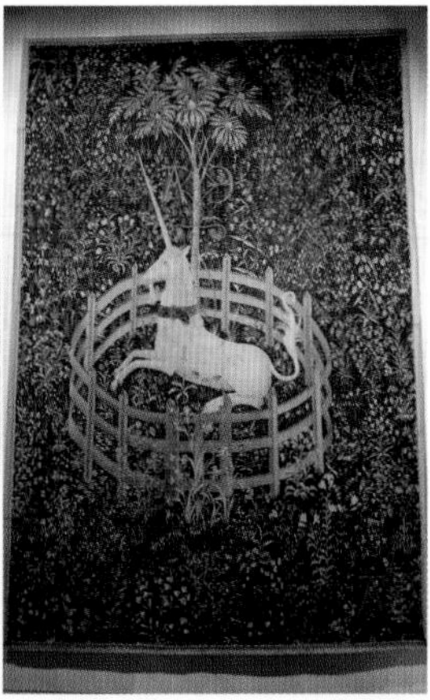

One of the set of late 15th-century Flemish Unicorn tapestries on display at The Cloisters

FLUSHING MEADOWS– CORONA PARK

nycgovparks.org

Queens' largest park has recreation facilities, the interactive New York Hall of Science (47-01 111th Street, tel 718/699-0005, nysci. org); the Queens Museum scale panorama of New York (New York Building, tel 718/592-9700, queensmuseum.org) and the Unisphere, the world's largest globe. Arthur Ashe Stadium hosts the US Open tennis tournament and the New York Mets play baseball at Citi Field.

➕ See map ▷ 111

HARLEM

This was the capital of black culture in America during the Harlem Renaissance in the 1920s. Music lovers should visit the Apollo Theater (253 W 125th Street, tel 212/531-5305, apollotheater.org) for big-name acts or the famous amateur showcase. You'll find historic exhibits mounted at the Schomburg Center for Research in Black Culture (515 Malcolm X Boulevard, tel 917/275-6975, nypl.org).

➕ See map ▷ 110

NEW YORK BOTANICAL GARDEN

nybg.org

America's largest city botanical center, this National Historic Landmark has 250 acres (101ha) of beautiful displays every season. Floral extravaganzas, a fascinating conservatory and old growth trees are among the wonders.

➕ See map ▷ 111 ✉ 2900 Southern Boulevard, Bronx ☎ 718/817-8700 🕐 Tue–Sun 10–6 💲 Expensive

ROOSEVELT ISLAND

It costs just a subway token for the 5-minute tram ride over the East River to Roosevelt Island for exciting architecture and city views. The futuristic campus of Cornell Tech (tech.cornell.edu) is still in progress but already a showpiece. A riverside path with non-stop city vistas leads to Franklin D. Roosevelt Four Freedoms Park (FDRfourseasonspark.org), a tribute to the late president.

➕ See map ▷ 110

YANKEE STADIUM

yankees.mlb.com

The New York Yankees have been one of the most successful baseball teams in US history, since Babe Ruth joined them in 1920 and became a hero. Attending a game is a strong part of local culture and makes for a great night out.

➕ See map ▷ 111 ✉ E 161st Street, Bronx ☎ Tickets 877/469-9849 🕐 Season runs Apr–Oct. Check schedule for games 🍴 Concession stands 🚇 4, B, D 161st Street/Yankee Stadium 💲 Expensive

The Yankee Stadium in the Bronx, home of the New York Yankees

City Tours

This section contains self-guided tours that will help you explore the sights in each of the city's regions. Each tour is designed to take a day, with a map pinpointing the recommended places along the way. There is a quick reference guide at the end of each tour, listing everything you need in that region, so you know exactly what's close by.

CITY TOURS

Lower Manhattan

The cradle of New York, Lower Manhattan is steeped in history—new immigrants landed here from the 17th century until the early 20th century. This area is also home to the Financial District, historic Seaport and fashionable SoHo.

Morning
Start the day at the tip of Manhattan in **Battery Park** (▷ 66), with its splendid views of New York Harbor. Ferries for the **Statue of Liberty** (▷ 54–55) and **Ellis Island** (▷ 26–27) leave from Castle Clinton, but save these for a separate day. Cross State Street to admire the beautiful Beaux Arts facade of the **US Custom House** (▷ 73), housing the National Museum of the American Indian. Then proceed along Bowling Green, the small square opposite, past the Charging Bull statue (right), a symbol of Wall Street.

Mid-morning
Walk up Broadway and note the plaques for more than a century of ticker-tape parades. Continue north to visit the **World Trade Center** (▷ 62–63). Farther south, **Trinity Church** (left; ▷ 59) marks the west end of **Wall Street** (▷ 58–59); stroll around the old churchyard, then head down Wall Street to **Federal Hall**, the **New York Stock Exchange** and other sites.

Lunch
Rub shoulders with Financial District workers and have a pub lunch at **The Bailey** (▷ 142), one block north of Wall Street. Try a hearty *plat du jour* such as shepherd's pie or fish and chips, or visit the new **Eataly Downtown** (4 World Trade Center).

Afternoon

Walk north on Front Street to **South Street Seaport** (▷ 72). From the waterfront along the East River there are good views of **Brooklyn Bridge** (▷ 66). Follow Dover Street west to **City Hall** (▷ 67), then take Centre Street north into **Chinatown** (left; ▷ 20–21). Explore its bustling markets, quiet temples and herbalist shops. Discover the culture of this area with a stop at the **Museum of Chinese in America** (▷ 70), which details the experiences of these immigrants.

Mid-afternoon

Chinatown spills north into **Little Italy**. Walk north on Mulberry Street, and when you reach **St. Patrick's Old Cathedral** (▷ 72), turn left on Prince Street, which will bring you into **SoHo** (▷ 52–53). Grab a coffee from one of the many cafés around here to keep you going as you admire the cast-iron buildings and indulge in some shopping, from Nike to Yves Saint-Laurent. Most stores here stay open well into early evening.

CITY TOURS

Evening

There are plenty of ultra-chic bars in SoHo for a cocktail or nightcap. For some old SoHo atmosphere, try **Fanelli's** (right; 94 Prince Street, between Mercer and Greene streets, tel 212/226-9412).

Dinner

There's been a pub on the site of **Fraunces Tavern** (54 Pearl Street, tel 212/968-1776) since the late 18th century, or head east to **Delicatessen** (▷ 144), for updated versions of comfort food. There's great SoHo people-watching from the outdoor tables. For quintessential New York pizza, go to **Lombardi's** (32 Spring Street at Mott Street, tel 212/941-7994). It was the first sit-down pizzeria in America.

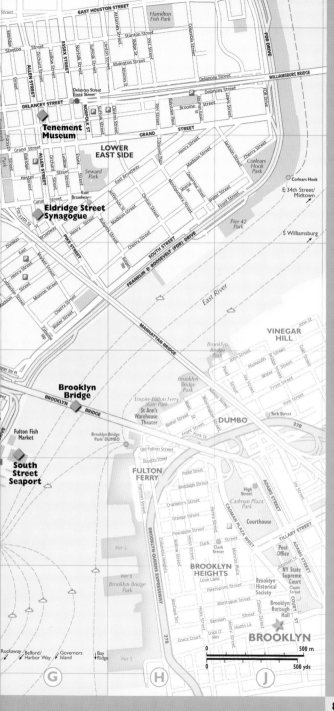

EAST HOUSTON STREET

Hamilton
Fish Park

Stanton Street

Rivington Street

ESSEX STREET

Delancey Street
Essex Street

WILLIAMSBURG BRIDGE

FDR DRIVE

Delancey Street

DELANCEY STREET

**Tenement
Museum**

NORFOLK ST

Broome Street

GRAND STREET

Henry Street

Corlears
Hook
Park

Madison Street

**LOWER
EAST SIDE**

Seward
Park

East Broadway

○ Corlears Hook

East Broadway

Cherry Street

Water Street

Front Street

E 34th Street/
Midtown

**Eldridge Street
Synagogue**

Pike Street

Pier 42
Park

ALLEN STREET

Henry Street

S Williamsburg

Madison Street

SOUTH STREET

Canal Street

FRANKLIN D. ROOSEVELT (FDR) DRIVE

Henry Street

Monroe Street

Cherry Street

Water Street

East River

MANHATTAN BRIDGE

**VINEGAR
HILL**

John St

Brooklyn
Bridge Park

John Street

Plymouth Street

Cold Spring

Water Street

Front Street

**Brooklyn
Bridge**

Brooklyn
Bridge Park

Empire-Fulton Ferry
State Park

St Ann's
Warehouse
Theater

BROOKLYN BRIDGE

Water Street

Front Street

York Street

DUMBO

○ York Street

278

Fulton Fish
Market

Brooklyn Bridge
Park/ DUMBO

Old Fulton Street

**South
Street
Seaport**

Doughty Street

**FULTON
FERRY**

Poplar Street

Middagh Street

High
Street

ADAMS STREET

Cranberry Street

Henry Street

Cadman Plaza
Park

Courthouse

Orange Street

CADMAN PLAZA WEST

Pineapple Street

Clark Street

Clark
Street

Monroe Place

TILLARY STREET

BROOKLYN-QUEENS EXPRESSWAY

Willow Street

Columbia Heights

Pier 2

Love Lane

**BROOKLYN
HEIGHTS**

Pierrepont Street

Brooklyn
Historical
Society

Post
Office

NY State
Supreme
Court

COURT ST

Pier 3

Brooklyn Bridge
Park

Montague Street

Clinton Street

Court
Street

Hicks Street

Remsen Street

Brooklyn Borough
Hall

Montague Ter.

Grace Court

Grace Ct.
Alley

Henry Street

Hunts La.

★ **BROOKLYN**

Pier 5

278

Rockaway

Belford/
Harbor Way

Governors
Island

Bay
Ridge

0   500 m

0   500 yds

G   **H**   **J**

Lower Manhattan Quick Reference Guide

 TOP 25 SIGHTS AND EXPERIENCES

Chinatown (▷ 20)
Explore this bustling neighborhood of streetside produce stalls, herbalist shops, Buddhist temples, dim sum parlors and tempting restaurants.

Ellis Island (▷ 26)
Follow in the footsteps of millions of immigrants, most of whom traveled in cramped steerage class, who passed through this gateway to New York and the New World.

SoHo (▷ 52)
SoHo features unique boutiques, top clothing chains, several art galleries, fashionable bars and stylish restaurants, many in 19th-century cast-iron buildings.

Statue of Liberty (▷ 54)
A visit to this iconic landmark is a must on any trip to New York. The ferry ride to the island is impressive, and the view from the statue's crown is breathtaking.

Wall Street (▷ 58)
During Dutch colonial times, Wall Street marked the northern boundary of New York. Now home to bankers and brokers, it's the powerhouse of the US economy.

World Trade Center (▷ 62)
The National September 11 Memorial, on the site of the Twin Towers, is both impressive and poignant. It's a quiet place for peace and contemplation.

CITY TOURS

MORE TO SEE — 64

Battery Park
Brookfield Place
Brooklyn Bridge
City Hall
Eldridge Street Synagogue
Museum of Chinese in America
New Museum
St. Patrick's Old Cathedral
St. Paul's Chapel
South Street Seaport
Tenement Museum
US Custom House

SHOP — 114

Books
The Mysterious Bookshop
Clothes
Abercrombie & Fitch
Resurrection
Discount
Century 21

Food and Wine
The Pickle Guys
Homewares
New Kam Man

ENTERTAINMENT — 126

Bars
The Dead Rabbit Grocery and Grog
Parkside Lounge
The Porterhouse
    at Fraunces Tavern
Cinema
Film Forum

Clubs
Arlene's Grocery
SOB's
Comedy
Comedy Cellar
Live Music
City Winery

EAT — 138

Asian
Mission Chinese Food
Oriental Garden
Casual
The Bailey
Bubby's
Delicatessen

Classic NY
Katz's Deli
The Odeon
Fine Dining
Delmonico's
Manhatta

Downtown and Chelsea

The area from Houston Street north to 30th Street encompasses NoHo and the East Village, the tree-lined streets of Greenwich Village, the Meatpacking District with its fashionable stores and clubs, and Chelsea, home of the High Line and the Whitney Museum of American Art.

Morning

Start the day with breakfast at one of the bakeries in **Chelsea Market** (right; ▷ 120). You can either eat there or take it with you up to the **High Line** (▷ 40–41). Begin your explorations by heading north to **Hudson Yards** (▷ 68). Later, find your way back to the Gansevoort Street-end of the High Line and the **Whitney Museum of American Art** (▷ 60–61).

Late morning/lunch

Leave the High Line at its southern terminus and strike out for the heart of **Greenwich Village** (▷ 36–37) along Bleecker Street. If you are in need a snack, you'll pass the famous **Magnolia Bakery** (401 Bleecker Street) and **Gran Gelato** (335 Bleeker Street). When Bleecker Street reaches MacDougal Street, head north. These blocks were the epicenter of the early 1960s folk scene. You'll soon reach **Washington Square** (▷ 73) which is a great place to sit and do a bit of people-watching. But first, lunch—the bistro-style **North Square** restaurant (▷ 147) in the **Washington Square Hotel** (▷ 159) is a good choice for Mediterranean dishes.

Afternoon

After lunch, stroll through Washington Square to its southern side (West 4th Street) and begin walking east to the **East Village** (▷ 24–25). The **Merchant's House Museum** (left) is a fascinating look back at an earlier era, complete with furnishings that were moved into the house in the 1830s. Then make your way up to **St. Mark's Place** (E 8th Street) with its lively mix of ethnic restaurants and funky shops.

Late afternoon

From the East Village head back to Broadway and the **Strand Bookstore** (▷ 125) and **Grace Church**, which has free audio tours via cell phone. Just a few blocks north of the church is **Union Square** (left; ▷ 73). Visit on a Monday, Wednesday, Friday or Saturday, and you'll be able to browse the food stands of **Union Square Greenmarket** (▷ 125, panel).

Evening

For a historic watering hole, head for the **White Horse Tavern** (▷ 137) on Hudson Street, where poet Dylan Thomas drank his last. Or head up to 23rd Street: At Fifth Avenue is **Eataly** (▷ 121), which has imported Italian goods and fine restaurants. It stands in the shadow of the **Flatiron Building** (▷ 68), New York's best early skyscraper.

Dinner

If you're not dining at Eataly, head a few blocks north to **Pondicheri** (▷ 148), a sophisticated take on classic Indian dishes with an emphasis on sharing.

Late evening

After dinner, you are spoiled for choice. Return to the Meatpacking District (right) or head back to the West Village for jazz at the **Blue Note** (▷ 132) or the **Village Vanguard** (178 7th Avenue South at W 11th Street, tel 212/255-4037). The clubs on Bleecker and MacDougal Street feature live music, too, with **Le Poisson Rouge** (158 Bleecker Street, tel 212/505-3474) drawing a wide range of acts, from classical trios to world music to cult bands.

Pier 79-
Midtown W 39th St

LINCOLN TUNNEL 495

West 39th Street
West 38th Street
West 37th Street
West 36th Street
West 35th Street

GARMENT
DISTRICT

⑫ Pier 76

Jacob Javits
Convention
Center

11TH AVENUE

12TH AVENUE

9A

7TH AVENUE

8th Avenue

Broadway

Macy's

34th Street
Penn Station

WEST 34TH STREET

34th Street/
Hudson Yards

34th Street
Penn Station

34th Street
Herald Square

West 33rd Street

West 31st Street

Madison
Square
Garden

PENN
STATION

⑬

The Vessel

Hudson
Yards

West 30th Street

WEST 30TH STREET

West 30th Street

West 29th Street

West 28th Street

West 30th
Street
Heliport

Chelsea
Park

Pier 66

11th
Avenue

10th
Avenue

9th
Avenue

8th
Avenue

7th
Avenue

West 27th Street

Chelsea
Gallery
District

West 26th Street

West 25th Street

MANHATTAN

Pier 64

⑭

High Line

West 24th Street

CHELSEA

23rd Street

23rd Street

West 2
23rd Stre

Chelsea
Waterside
Park

West 23rd Street

West 22nd Street

Pier 62

West 21st Street

West 20th Street

Chelsea Hotel

Pier 61

West 19th Street

Pier 60

⑮

Chelsea Piers

Pier 59

West 18th Street

18th Street

Hudson River Park

West 17th Street

Rubin Museum
of Art

West 16th Street

Chelsea Market

MEATPACKING
DISTRICT

Pier 57

WEST 15TH STREET

14th Street

14th Street

14

WEST 14TH STREET

8th Avenue

6th Aven

Washington
Street

13th
Street

WEST
VILLAGE

Village
Vanguard

Whitney Museum
of American Art

Pier 54

West 12th Street

Little West
12th Street

⑯

Gansevoort Peninsula Park
under construction
due to open 2023

Horatio Street

Jane Street

Magnolia
Bakery

Pier 51

Bethune Street

White Horse
Tavern

West 11th Street

Christopher Street
Sheridan Square

West Washingt

Bank
Street

Hudson River Park

Gran
Gelato

⑰

Hudson River

GREENWICH
VILLAGE

Pier 46

Charles
Street

West 10th Street

Barrow Street

Pier 45

Morton Street

Leroy Street

⑱

West Houston Street

Houston
Street

Children's
Museum
of the Arts

Pier 40

New York City
Fire Museum

Ⓑ   Ⓒ   Ⓓ

Downtown and Chelsea
Quick Reference Guide

CITY TOURS

East Village and NoHo (▷ 24)
The East Village, with its immigrant history and counterculture vibe, is well worth exploring. Nearby NoHo, once one of the most elegant residential neighborhoods in the city, still features beautiful homes and cobblestone streets.

Greenwich Village (▷ 36)
Once an actual village, this area has gorgeous, tree-lined streets. It was the center of the folk revival of the 1960s and birthplace of the gay rights movement, and has been home to generations of artists and writers.

High Line (▷ 40)
Local residents banded together to turn this abandoned elevated railbed into one of New York's premier parks. Watch for the Plinth, inspired by London's Trafalgar Square Fourth Plinth, with its commissioned art.

Whitney Museum of American Art (▷ 60)
One of the finest collections of 20th-century American art. Enjoy stimulating temporary exhibitions alongside works from the outstanding permanent collection.

Midtown

Midtown is a must for visitors. It has leading museums, pulsating Times Square, Grand Central Terminal plus the magnet for shoppers—Fifth Avenue. It also has three of New York's most famous skyscrapers, two with observatories for stupendous views.

Morning

Get an early start at **Rockefeller Center** (▷ 50–51). The subway concourse below 30 Rockefeller Plaza is full of restaurants, cafés and delis; pick up a coffee and breakfast sandwich, or have a more substantial meal at the **Rock Center Café**, which looks out on the famous ice rink or summer gardens. Be sure to see the many beautiful artworks around the complex, before or after enjoying the observation decks at **Top of the Rock** (right) for majestic city views.

Mid-morning

Walk west along 50th Street to **Radio City Music Hall** (▷ 136), and turn right up Sixth Avenue. Turn right on 53rd Street to visit the **Museum of Modern Art** (▷ 46–47).

Lunch

"Quick" and "inexpensive" are foreign words in this part of Midtown. Your best bet for a simple lunch that won't break the bank is to head to the **Halal Guys**, who operate their renowned food carts at the corner of 53rd Street and Avenue of the Americas. Other good-value options are **Dim Sum Palace** (47 West 55th Street) and **pizzArte** (69 West 55th Street).

Afternoon

Walk east to **Fifth Avenue** (▷ 30–31) and let the shopping spree begin—even if you're just window shopping and ogling the fabulous displays. If you enter only one store, make it **Saks Fifth Avenue** (▷ 125); the perfume and cosmetic counters fill the first floor. Just north is the beautiful **St. Patrick's Cathedral** (▷ 71).

Mid-afternoon

Turn east on 45th Street and walk to the Park Avenue entrance of **Grand Central Terminal** (▷ 34–35). Admire its stunning main concourse, then head for a welcome rest and a snack in the **Dining Concourse** (▷ 145, panel). Exit on 42nd Street, and detour one block east to step into the art-deco lobby of the **Chrysler Building** (▷ 67). Then walk west on 42nd Street to Fifth Avenue, and visit the **New York Public Library** (left; ▷ 48–49).

Evening

As dusk falls, continue west and turn right up Broadway into **Times Square** (▷ 56–57), in all its neon glory. Head for the **TKTS booth** (▷ 56), where you may get a discount ticket for a Broadway show.

Dinner

Times Square is notorious for chain restaurants, but a good choice for real New York fare is **John's Pizzeria** (▷ 146). There's a branch of **Carmine's** at 200 W 44th Street, off Times Square.

Late evening

Afterward, take in that Broadway show, and/or grab a cab to end the evening with the best night-cap of all: the view of the twinkling lights of Manhattan from the top of the **Empire State Building** (right; ▷ 28–29).

Columbus
Circle

Coliseum
Park

Time
Warner
Center

59th Street/
Columbus Circle

The Pond

5th A
59th

Central Park South

(9) West 58th St

West 58th Street

P

Museum of Arts
and Design

57th Street

WEST 57TH STREET

WEST 57TH STREET

Carnegie
Hall

57th Street

P

West 56th Street

P P

West 56th Street

MIDTOWN

pizzArte

6th Avenue

Dim Sum
Palace

West 55th Street

West 55th Street

Spyscape

P

Museum of
Modern Art (MoMA)

West 54th Street

Columbus Avenue

5th Avenue

West 53rd Street

Halal Guys

7th Avenue

P

West 52nd Street

5th Avenue/
53rd Street

(10) West 52nd Street

P

West 52nd Street

St Pat
Cath

West 51st Street

9th Avenue

West 51st Street

Radio City
Music Hall

P

50th Street

50th Street

7th Avenue

8th Avenue

49th Street

Rockefeller
Center

Rock Center
Café

West 50th Street

West 49th Street

West 49th Street

47th-50th Streets
Rockefeller Ctr

West 48th Street

West 48th Street

P

P

THEATER
DISTRICT

P

P

West 47th Street

West 47th Street

P

West 46th Street

TKTS booth

West 46th Street

P

Times
Square

Fifth Avenue

(11) West 45th Street

P

National
Geographic
Encounter:
Ocean Odyssey

West 45th Street

P

West 44th Street

P

West 44th Street

John's
Pizzeria

P

Carmine's

MIDTOWN

Gulliver's
Gate

P

West 43rd Street

West 43rd Street

P

42nd Street/
Port Authority
Bus Terminal

Reuters
Building

Times Square
42nd Street

42nd Street
Bryant Park

5th A

WEST 42ND STREET

WEST 42ND STREET

Port Authority
Bus Terminal

P

New
Amsterdam
Theater

New York
Public
Library

5th A

West 40th Street

P

Bryant
Park

West 40th Street

West 39th Street

8th Avenue

7th Avenue

Broadway

6th Avenue

West 39th Street

5th Avenue

(12) West 38th Street

West 38th Street

9th Avenue

West 37th Street

GARMENT
DISTRICT

West 37th Street

KOREATOWN

P

West 36th Street

West 36th Street

West 35th Street

West 35th Street

P

34th Street
Penn Station

Macy's

WEST 34TH STREET

34th Street
Herald Square

WEST 34TH STREET

West 33rd Street

34th Street
Penn Station

34th Street

Empire State
Building

West 33rd Street

(13) Moynihan Train Hall
under construction
due to open 2021

Madison
Square
Garden

PENN
STATION

West 32nd Street

MIDTOWN SOU

West 31st Street

West 31st Street

P

(C)

West 30th Street

(D)

West 30th Street

P

P

East 60th Street

Lexington Avenue/59th Street

59th Street

Forty Carrots

EAST 59TH STREET
SUTTON PLACE

th Street

East 58th Street

th Street

57TH STREET

EAST 57TH STREET

th Street

East 56th Street

th Street

East 55th Street

th Street

MIDTOWN EAST

East 54th Street

Lexington Avenue/
53rd Street

**Lipstick
Building**

East 53rd Street

3rd Street

**TURTLE
BAY**

Seagram
Building

East 52nd Street

*Peter
Detmold
Park*

2nd St

51st
Street

East 51st Street

1st St

East 50th Street

0th St

3RD AVENUE

2ND AVENUE

1ST AVENUE

Park Avenue

Lexington Avenue

East 49th Street

0th St

East 48th Street

8th St

East 47th Street

7th Street

East 46th Street

5th Street

East 45th Street

**United Nations
Headquarters**

5th St

Grand
Central
Terminal

East 44th Street

East River

St

**TUDOR
CITY**

East 43rd Street

42ND ST

**Chrysler
Building**

EAST 42ND STREET

42nd Street -
Grand Central

Chanin
Building

**Daily News
Building**

East 41st Street

1st Street

0th Street

MURRAY HILL

East 40th Street

East 39th Street

FRANKLIN D. ROOSEVELT (FDR) DRIVE

9th St

8th St

3RD AVENUE

2ND AVENUE

1ST AVENUE

Park Avenue

Lexington Avenue

East 38th Street

7th St

**Morgan Library
& Museum**

6th Street

5th Street

East 35th Street

East 34th Street/
Midtown East

34TH STREET

EAST 34TH STREET

3rd Street

33rd Street

East 33rd Street

East
34th Street
Heliport

2nd Street

0

500 m

0

500 yds

31st St

Park Avenue S

KIPS BAY

East 30th Street

Ⓕ

Ⓖ

Midtown Quick Reference Guide

 SIGHTS AND EXPERIENCES

Empire State Building (▷ 28)
The most famous New York skyscraper affords panoramic views
over Manhattan by day or night.

Fifth Avenue (▷ 30)
For high fashion, style and quality,
there's no better place to shop
than Fifth Avenue.

Grand Central Terminal (▷ 34)
Some half a million people pass
through this stunning Beaux Arts
concourse every day.

Museum of Modern Art (▷ 46)
From 19th-century masterpieces
to contemporary art, this is one of
the city's leading museums.

New York Public Library (▷ 48)
See the fine carved ceiling and the
glorious reading rooms of this
Beaux Arts landmark.

Rockefeller Center (▷ 50)
Admire the plaza and artworks of
this urban complex, then take in
the view from the Top of the Rock.

Times Square (▷ 56)
Come here at night to see the wall
of neon at the heart of New York's
famous Theater District or browse
in its megastores by day.

CITY TOURS

MORE TO SEE | 64

Chrysler Building
Gulliver's Gate
Morgan Library & Museum
National Geographic Encounter: Ocean Odyssey
St. Patrick's Cathedral
Spyscape
United Nations Headquarters

SHOP | 114

Clothes
Brooks Brothers
Dolce & Gabbana
Nordstrom
Thomas Pink
Department Stores
Bergdorf Goodman
Macy's

Saks Fifth Avenue
Shoes
Manolo Blahnik
Sports Goods
Niketown New York
Technology
Apple Store

ENTERTAINMENT | 126

Bars
Four Seasons Hotel TY Bar
Classical Music
Carnegie Hall
Jazz
Birdland
Live Music
Madison Square Garden
PlayStation Theater

Theater/Performance
The New Victory Theater
New World Stages
Radio City Music Hall
Roundabout Theater Company
Signature Theatre

EAT | 138

Asian
Kajitsu
Nobu Fifty Seven
Casual
Forty Carrots
Grand Central Terminal
John's Pizzeria
Classic NY
'21' Club
Oyster Bar
Sarge's Deli

Fine Dining
Le Bernardin
Casa Lever
Per Se
Greek
Uncle Nick's

CITY TOURS

95

Upper East Side and Central Park

Central Park is a huge green space accessible to all New Yorkers. The museums of the Upper East Side, facing the park along Fifth Avenue, are renowned worldwide. Their collections range from priceless antiquities to modern art, design, ethnic culture and history.

Morning

It's unlikely you'll visit more than two museums in a day. This tour will take you past the most popular, and give you a taste of Central Park in between. Most museums don't open until 10am, so start with an early morning stroll in **Central Park** (left; ▷ 18–19). Enter at the southeast corner by Grand Army Plaza (E 59th Street and Fifth Avenue). A pedestrian path (just in from Fifth Avenue) leads to the zoo. If you follow the paved road, first detour to the Pond, with lovely views of the skyline, before reaching the Dairy Visitor Center, where you can pick up a park map. Continue north along The Mall, lined with one of the largest stands of elm trees in America. The southern end, Literary Walk, has statues of famous writers.

Mid-morning

Continue through the park to the Bethesda Terrace and Fountain (right), overlooking the Lake. Admire the view, then take the pedestrian walkway beneath the terrace—look up to see the Minton tile ceiling, designed by British architect Jacob Wrey Mould. Follow the lakeside path to your right. At Loeb Boathouse veer right to the Conservatory Water, the pretty model boat pond. You may want to detour at E 75th Street to see the treasures of the **Frick Collection** (▷ 32–33), now housed at the Breuer Museum on Madison Avenue.

Lunch

The Met, Guggenheim, Cooper Hewitt and Neue Galerie all have cafés. In Central Park, **The Loeb Boathouse** restaurant (▷ 146) has an express café as well as formal dining on the terrace. Alternatively, picnic on the Great Lawn behind the Met.

Afternoon
A visit to the **Metropolitan Museum of Art** (left; ▷ 44–45) is worthwhile. It stands right in Central Park. Try to catch a free tour of the museum's highlights (times vary). At Fifth Avenue and 86th Street is the **Neue Galerie** (▷ 70). Farther north at 89th Street is the **Guggenheim Museum** (▷ 38–39), housed in Frank Lloyd Wright's stunning circular building. Beyond is the **Cooper Hewitt Smithsonian Design Museum** (▷ 22–23) and the **Jewish Museum** (▷ 69). Across Fifth Avenue in Central Park is the famous Reservoir. The running track and bridle path around the Reservoir are good places to stroll.

Evening
In summer, Central Park has evening events (Shakespeare in the Park; concerts on the Great Lawn), but be aware of your surroundings when in the park after dark. If a museum has a late night, evenings are a good time to visit, or head for a cocktail at upscale **Bemelmans Bar** (Carlyle Hotel, 35 E 76th Street, tel 212/744-1600).

Dinner
The superb (and pricey) French cuisine at nearby **Café Boulud** (▷ 143) makes it a good choice for dinner.

Late evening
Return to Carlyle Hotel's **Café Carlyle** (▷ 132) for jazz and cabaret.

West 92nd Street
(4)
West 91st St

Jewish Museum
East 91st Street

West 90th Street

Cooper Hewitt Smithsonian Design Museum

West 89th Street

Guggenheim Museum
East 89th Street

West 88th Street

East 88th Street

West 87th Street

86th Street

East 87th Street

Jacqueline Kennedy Onassis Reservoir

West 86th St
(5)

86th Street Transverse

Neue Galerie
East 86th Stre

West 85th Street

Central Park

East 85th Stre

West 84th Street

Arthur Ross Pinetum

East 84th Stre

West 83rd Street

Summit Rock

The Great Lawn

Metropolitan Museum of Art

West 82nd Street

East 82nd Stre

81st Street (Museum of Natural History)

Delacorte Theater

Cleopatra's Needle

East 81st Stre

West 81st Street

Theodore Roosevelt Park

East 80th Stre

Turtle Pond

Belvedere Castle

American Museum of Natural History
(6)

79th Street Transverse

East 79th Stre

East 78th Stre

New-York Historical Society

Central Park West

The Ramble

Cedar Hill

East 77th Stre

West 77th Street

Café Carlyle, Bemelman's Bar

West 75th Street

Café Boul

The San Remo

Ladies Pavilion

The Loeb Boathouse

East 75th Stre

Frick Collection

West 74th Street

The Lake

East 74th Stre

West 73rd Street

East 73rd Stre

The Dakota
(7)

Central Park Driveway

Cherry Hill

Bethesda Terrace

Conservatory Water

East 72nd Stre

West 72nd Street

Strawberry Fields

72nd Street Transverse

Rumsey Playfield

East Green

East 71st Stree

Frick Mansion

West 71st Street

72nd Street

Naumburg Bandshell

East 70th Stre

E 70

West 70th Street

Columbus Avenue

West 69th Street

Madison Avenue

East 69th Stre

West 68th Street

Sheep Meadow

The Mall

East 68th Stre

West 67th Street

Central Park

Literary Walk

East 67th Str

West 66th St
(8)

Tavern on the Green

Tisch Children's Zoo

East 66th Str

66th Street Lincoln Center

W 65th Street

65th Street Transverse

Central Park Zoo

East 65th Str

West 64th St

BROADWAY

Dairy Visitor Center

East 64th Str

Heckscher Ballfields

East 63rd Str

Wollman Skating Rink

West 62nd Street

East 62nd Str

Columbus Avenue

East 61st Str

West Drive

Central Park Drive

East Drive

The Pond

5th Avenue/ 59th Street

Time Warner Center
(9)

East 60th Str

Coliseum Park

Columbus Circle

59th Street Columbus Circle

C

Central

Park

South

D

E 59th

E

W 58th Street

West 58th Street

5th Avenue

East 92nd Street
East 91st Street
East 90th Street
East 89th Street
East 88th Street
East 87th Street
East 86th Street
East 85th Street
East 84th Street
East 83rd Street
East 82nd Street
East 81st Street
East 80th Street
East 79th Street
East 78th Street
East 77th Street
East 76th Street
East 75th Street
East 74th Street
East 73rd Street
East 72nd Street
East 71st Street
East 70th Street
East 69th Street
East 68th Street
East 67th Street
East 66th Street
East 65th Street
East 64th Street
EAST 63RD STREET
EAST 62ND STREET
East 61st Street
EAST 59TH STREET
East 58th Street

Lexington Avenue
3RD AVENUE
2ND AVENUE
1ST AVENUE
York Avenue
East End Avenue
FRANKLIN D. ROOSEVELT (FDR) DRIVE
YORK AVENUE

86th Street
86th Street
77th Street
72nd Street
68th Street Hunter College

Lexington Avenue/ 63rd Street
Lexington Avenue/ 59th Street
59th Street

UPPER EAST SIDE
LENOX HILL
SUTTON PLACE

ia Society d Museum
enter llege

Carl Schurz Park
Soundview

East 90th Street

CITY TOURS

East River

Rockefeller University

Roosevelt Island

Road 5

Roosevelt Island Aerial Tramway
QUEENSBORO BRIDGE

St Catherine's Park

0   250 m
0   250 yds

N

F   G   H

Upper East Side and Central Park
Quick Reference Guide

Central Park (▷ 18)
This great, green expanse is a visionary creation in the heart of the city. Join New Yorkers as they walk, jog, cycle, row, picnic, stroll with their dogs, play ball and escape the urban buzz.

Cooper Hewitt Smithsonian Design Museum (▷ 22)
An eclectic mix of old-school and cutting-edge, the superb exhibits and permanent collections of decorative arts and furniture in the Carnegie mansion are stunning.

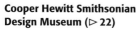

Frick Collection (▷ 32)
Henry Clay Frick's magnificent collection of old masters and decorative arts is temporarily housed at the Breuer building while its original mansion home is being expanded.

Guggenheim Museum (▷ 38)
Frank Lloyd Wright's ground-breaking, nautilus-shaped building with its internal spiral walkway gets all the glory, but the collection of late19th- and 20th-century art is also worth a look.

Metropolitan Museum of Art (▷ 44)
Don't be daunted by the sheer vastness of this fabulous art museum. Viewing just one or two of its wonderful collections will leave lasting memories.

MORE TO SEE   64

Jewish Museum
Met Breuer
El Museo del Barrio
Museum of the City of New York
Neue Galerie

SHOP   114

Books
Kitchen Arts and Letters
Clothes
Calvin Klein
Ralph Lauren

Department Stores
Bloomingdale's
Swimwear
Malia Mills

ENTERTAINMENT   126

Bars
Auction House
Comedy
Dangerfield's
Jazz
Café Carlyle

Literary Events/Readings
92nd Street Y
Theater/Performance
Florence Gould Hall
Shakespeare in the Park

EAT   138

Casual
Jackson Hole
Classic NY
The Loeb Boathouse
Fine Dining
Daniel

French
Café Boulud
Middle Eastern
A La Turka
Persepolis

Upper West Side

The area west of Central Park is a largely residential, pleasantly leafy neighborhood of grand apartment buildings and big brownstones. Its major attractions are Lincoln Center and the wonderful American Museum of Natural History.

Morning
Start at **Lincoln Center** (▷ 42–43). Walk around the plaza, admiring the Revson Fountain, the Metropolitan Opera House and other cultural venues. Guided tours are available from the David Rubenstein Atrium across Broadway. From the northeast corner of the Lincoln Center, cross over the intersection with Broadway to the **American Folk Art Museum** (left; ▷ 66). Continue up Columbus Avenue, taking in its shops and restaurants. If you're ready for a snack, you'll pass the **Magnolia Bakery** (200 Columbus Avenue)—it's never too early for one of their cupcakes.

Mid-morning
Turn right on W 72nd Street. On the corner with Central Park West is the Dakota, the first luxury co-op apartment building on the Upper West Side. Its most famous resident, former Beatle John Lennon, was fatally shot outside the south gate in 1980. Cross over the road to enter **Central Park** (▷ 18–19), and follow the path to **Strawberry Fields**, where the black-and-white *Imagine* mosaic (right) is the centerpiece of a garden and memorial to John Lennon. From here there is a good view of the Dakota Apartments and the towers of the neighboring San Remo Apartments. Back on Central Park West is the **New-York Historical Society** (▷ 71). Then head west to Broadway.

Lunch

Broadway is another great shopping street. Continue north to 80th Street, where you can put together a picnic from the gourmet fare at **Zabar's** (right; ▷ 125), or get a sandwich at their adjoining café. Take it to **Riverside Park**, two blocks west, with views over the Hudson River.

Afternoon

Plan to spend the entire afternoon at the **American Museum of Natural History** (▷ 14–15). Highlights include the dinosaur halls, the animal dioramas and the Rose Center for Earth and Space (left).

Dinner

You won't have too much further to walk for an early dinner at **Blossom on Columbus** (▷ 143), the uptown outpost of this beloved vegetarian mini-chain, which emphasizes seasonal ingredients.

Evening

End where you started by retracing your steps back to **Lincoln Center** (right). Even if you haven't got tickets for an evening performance, a walk through the lit-up plaza is a magical way to end the day.

④

West 90th Street
West 89th Street
West 88th Street
West 87th Street
West 86th Street
West 85th Street
West 84th Street
West 83rd Street
West 82nd Street
West 81st Street
West 80th Street
West 79th Street
West 78th Street
West 77th Street
West 76th Street
West 75th Street
West 74th Street
West 73rd Street
West 72nd Street
West 71st Street
West 70th Street
West 69th Street
West 68th Street
West 67th Street
West 66th Street
West 65th Street
West 64th Street
West 63rd Street
West 62nd Street
West 61st Street
West 60th Street
West 59th Street
West 58th Street
WEST 57TH STREET

HENRY HUDSON PARKWAY

Riverside Drive

BROADWAY

Amsterdam Avenue

Columbus Avenue

Central Park West

86th Street

⑤

86th Street

Blossom on Columbus

Riverside Park

Zabar's

79th Street

81st Street (Museum of Natural History)

Theodore Roosevelt Park

American Museum of Natural History

New-York Historical Society

⑥

Hudson River

The San Remo

West End Avenue

Riverside Drive

Ansonia Building

72nd Street

The Dakota

⑦

UPPER WEST SIDE

72nd Street

Magnolia Bakery

Central Park West

American Folk Art Museum

Juilliard School

Lincoln Center

66th Street Lincoln Center

⑧

Freedom Place

Riverside Boulevard

JOE DIMAGGIO HIGHWAY

LINCOLN SQUARE

Damrosch Park

Fordham University Lincoln Center Campus

BROADWAY

Time Warner Center

59th St Columb

Coliseum Park

Columbus Circle

John Jay College of Criminal Justice

Museum of Arts and Design

⑨

Ⓐ Ⓑ Ⓒ

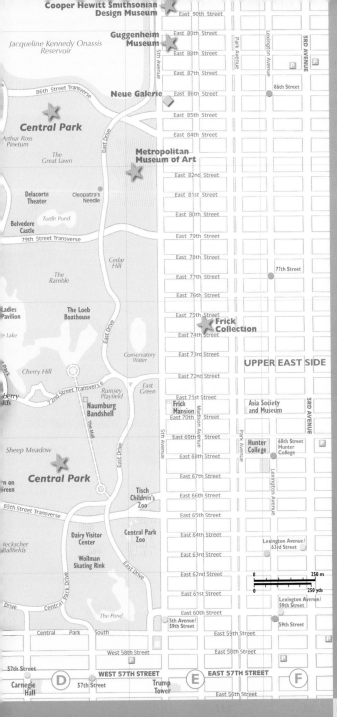

Cooper Hewitt Smithsonian
Design Museum

East 90th Street

East 89th Street

Guggenheim
Museum

East 88th Street

East 87th Street

Jacqueline Kennedy Onassis
Reservoir

86th Street Transverse

Neue Galerie

East 86th Street

East 85th Street

East 84th Street

Central Park

Arthur Ross
Pinetum

The
Great Lawn

Metropolitan
Museum of Art

East 82nd Street

Delacorte
Theater

Cleopatra's
Needle

East 81st Street

East 80th Street

Turtle Pond

Belvedere
Castle

79th Street Transverse

East 79th Street

East 78th Street

Cedar
Hill

East 77th Street

77th Street

The
Ramble

East 76th Street

East 75th Street

Ladies
Pavilion

The Loeb
Boathouse

East 74th Street

Frick
Collection

e Lake

Conservatory
Water

East 73rd Street

Cherry Hill

East 72nd Street

UPPER EAST SIDE

72nd Street Transverse

berry
ds

Rumsey
Playfield

East
Green

East 71st Street

Frick
Mansion

Naumburg
Bandshell

East 70th Street

Asia Society
and Museum

The Mall

East 69th Street

Sheep Meadow

East 68th Street

Hunter
College

68th Street
Hunter
College

Central Park

East 67th Street

n on
reen

East 66th Street

Tisch
Children's
Zoo

East 65th Street

65th Street Transverse

Dairy Visitor
Center

Central Park
Zoo

East 64th Street

leckscher
Ballfields

East 63rd Street

Lexington Avenue/
63rd Street

Wollman
Skating Rink

East 62nd Street

East 61st Street

0   250 m

0   250 yds

The Pond

East 60th Street

Lexington Avenue/
59th Street

5th Avenue/
59th Street

59th Street

Central   Park   South

East 59th Street

West 58th Street

East 58th Street

57th Street

West 57th Street

East 57th Street

Carnegie
Hall

57th Street

Trump
Tower

East 56th Street

D

E

F

CITY TOURS

105

SIGHTS AND EXPERIENCES

American Museum of Natural History (▷ 14)

This is the largest natural history museum in the world. The life-size, rearing Barosaurus in the main entrance hall leads to the renowned dinosaur halls, where fossil specimens of some of the earliest dinosaur discoveries are displayed. Add to that a priceless collection of gemstones, animal displays, the Rose Center for Earth and Space with its amazing planetarium, and more, and you could easily spend a whole day here.

Lincoln Center (▷ 42)

New York's premier performing arts complex is a sight to behold, with its gushing fountains and gleaming buildings, the huge arched windows and chandeliers of the Metropolitan Opera House, and the glowing lights reflected in its wide central plaza. In addition to housing the Metropolitan Opera, it is home to the New York Philharmonic, the Juilliard School of Music, the New York City Ballet and many others, and offers a vast array of entertainment.

View of Central Park West, including the Dakota and San Remo apartment buildings

CITY TOURS

Farther Afield

New York's outer boroughs are predominantly residential, but there is still plenty to see, especially in Brooklyn (▷ 16–17). With an early start, you can take in its top sights as well as two classic New York experiences.

Morning

Join the morning bustle of the city's commuters and begin your day at the tip of Manhattan at the Staten Island Ferry Terminal. The ferry ride (right) across Upper New York Bay is stunning in both directions and it's free. If you can, ride on the ferry's outside deck to get a good view of the Statue of Liberty—visible from the right side of the boat on the outward journey—and other sights. The round trip to and from Staten Island takes an hour; when you arrive you can catch the next ferry back to Manhattan. For a coffee and a late breakfast try The Gavel Grill, a block from the terminal at 9 Hyatt Street.

Mid-morning

Disembark and walk up Broadway to Bowling Green, where you can catch the No. 4 or 5 subway train to the Brooklyn Bridge/City Hall stop. On Park Row, a sidewalk entrance leads up to the wooden walkway of **Brooklyn Bridge** (left; ▷ 66). A walk (or jog) across the bridge is a must, and New Yorkers love it as much as visitors do. It's about a 20-minute walk, though it can take twice as long with stops to admire the views back to the Manhattan skyline.

Lunch
When you come to the end of the bridge, you'll have worked up an appetite so, when you see the DUMBO sign, take the stairwell down to the street and head toward the water. **Grimaldi's** (▷ 145) on Front Street has some of the best pizza in New York. Afterward, walk along the promenade for splendid vistas across the river to Manhattan.

Afternoon
Walk through the pretty brown-stone-lined streets of Brooklyn Heights to the Clark Street subway stop, and take No. 2 or 3 subway to the Eastern Parkway stop. This eastern side of Prospect Park contains two of Brooklyn's finest attractions: the **Brooklyn Museum** (right; ▷ 16–17) and **Brooklyn Botanic Garden** (990 Washington Avenue, tel 718/623-7200), with its rose garden, bonsai museum and Japanese Hill-and-Pond Garden. A visit to either could take up the afternoon.

Dinner
To get to Williamsburg and **Peter Luger Steak House** (▷ 148) for dinner, the quickest route is to take the No. 2 or 3 subway to Fulton Street in Manhattan and change to the J train to Marcy Avenue. If pricey red meat isn't your thing, stroll along Bedford Avenue, which is lined with inexpensive dining options.

Late evening
Williamsburg is filled with fun bars and live music. A good bet is the **Music Hall of Williamsburg** (66 N Sixth Street, tel 718/486-5400), which draws local talent, internationally known indie rockers, spoken-word artists and more. Or venture into neighboring Greenpoint to the **Black Rabbit** (91 Greenpoint Avenue, tel 718/349-1595), a local watering hole with a friendly vibe.

Teaneck
Englewood
80
Saddle Brook
19
20
46
Hackensack
Bogota
Garfield
PALISADES INT
Passaic
Hasbrouck Heights
Ridgefield Park
80
95
Clifton
21
17
Wallington
46
Palisades Park
Fort Lee
George Washington Bridge
3
Moonachie
Ridgefield
HENRY HUDSON PARK
Nutley
Rutherford
NEW JERSEY
3
95
Fairview
9
HARLEM
Lyndhurst
Hackensack River
95
Hudson River
NEW YORK
Belleville
North Arlington
1
West New York
Central Park
21
Secaucus
3
495
Weehawken
MANHATTAN
Kearny
NEW JERSEY TURNPIKE WESTERN SPUR
NEW JERSEY TURNPIKE EASTERN SPUR
Union City
57th St
Roosevelt Island
Lincoln Tunnel
280
Harrison
34th St
Queens Bridge
280
Hoboken
2nd Ave
280
9
14th St
East River
Newark
1
9A
FDR DRIVE
95
9
Jersey City
78
Holland Tunnel
1
Ellis Island
440
78
Liberty State Park
Manhattan Bridge
Newark Liberty International Airport
Hugh L. Carey Tunnel
Brooklyn Bridge
78
Governors Island
NEW JERSEY TURNPIKE
Statue of Liberty
278
Bayonne
440
Prospect Park
Brooklyn Botanic Garden
PROSPECT EXPY
Upper New York Bay
278
Newark Bay
BOROUGH PARK
440
Bayonne Bridge
278
OCEAN PARKWAY
PORT RICHMOND
CLIFTON
278
278
GRAVESEND
440
278
BELT PARKWAY
STATEN ISLAND
Verrazano Narrows Bridge
ARROCHAR
LIGHTHOUSE HILL
Lower New York Bay
Coney Island
LaTourette Park
Gateway National Recreation Area
GREAT KILLS

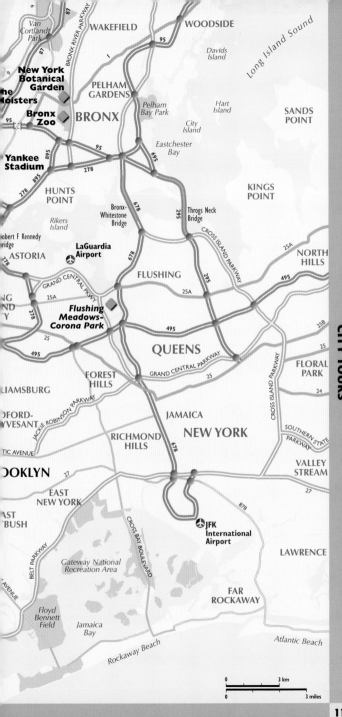

Van Cortlandt Park
WAKEFIELD
WOODSIDE
BRONX RIVER PARKWAY
95
Davids Island
Long Island Sound
New York Botanical Garden
The Cloisters
PELHAM GARDENS
Pelham Bay Park
Hart Island
SANDS POINT
Bronx Zoo
BRONX
City Island
Eastchester Bay
Yankee Stadium
95
695
278
KINGS POINT
895
HUNTS POINT
278
895
Rikers Island
Bronx-Whitestone Bridge
678
295
Throgs Neck Bridge
CROSS ISLAND PARKWAY
25A
NORTH HILLS
Robert F Kennedy Bridge
LaGuardia Airport
295
495
278
ASTORIA
GRAND CENTRAL PKWY
FLUSHING
25A
25A
678
ING
ND
TY
278
Flushing Meadows-Corona Park
495
495
25
25B
895
QUEENS
25
FLORAL PARK
495
FOREST HILLS
GRAND CENTRAL PARKWAY
25
24
LIAMSBURG
JACKIE ROBINSON PARKWAY
CROSS ISLAND PARKWAY
SOUTHERN STATE PARKWAY
FORD-
VESANT
JAMAICA
NEW YORK
TIC AVENUE
RICHMOND HILLS
678
VALLEY STREAM
OOKLYN
27
27
EAST NEW YORK
JFK International Airport
878
AST
BUSH
BELT PARKWAY
CROSS BAY BOULEVARD
LAWRENCE
AVENUE
Gateway National Recreation Area
FAR ROCKAWAY
Floyd Bennett Field
Jamaica Bay
Rockaway Beach
Atlantic Beach

| 0 | | 3 km |
| 0 | | 3 miles |

Farther Afield Quick Reference Guide

SIGHTS AND EXPERIENCES

Brooklyn (▷ 16–17)

If you've ever wondered what New York is like beyond Manhattan, Brooklyn is the best place to start. Brooklyn Heights is lined with classic brownstones, and the promenade offers perfect city views. You'll find The Brooklyn Museum here and the Sackler Center for Feminist Art. Alongside is the Brooklyn Botanic Garden. Walk back to Manhattan across the Brooklyn Bridge, a classic New York experience, or visit Williamsburg for its chic boutiques and bars, especially lively on weekends.

MORE TO SEE	64

Bronx Zoo
The Cloisters
Coney Island
Flushing Meadows–Corona Park

Harlem
New York Botanical Garden
Roosevelt Island
Yankee Stadium

SHOP	114

Vintage Clothing
Beacon's Closet

ENTERTAINMENT	126

Bars
Barbès
Union Hall

Live Music
Brooklyn Steel

EAT	138

Casual
Grimaldi's
Classic NY
Peter Luger Steak House

Contemporary
Blue Ribbon Brasserie
Henry's End
Fine Dining
River Café

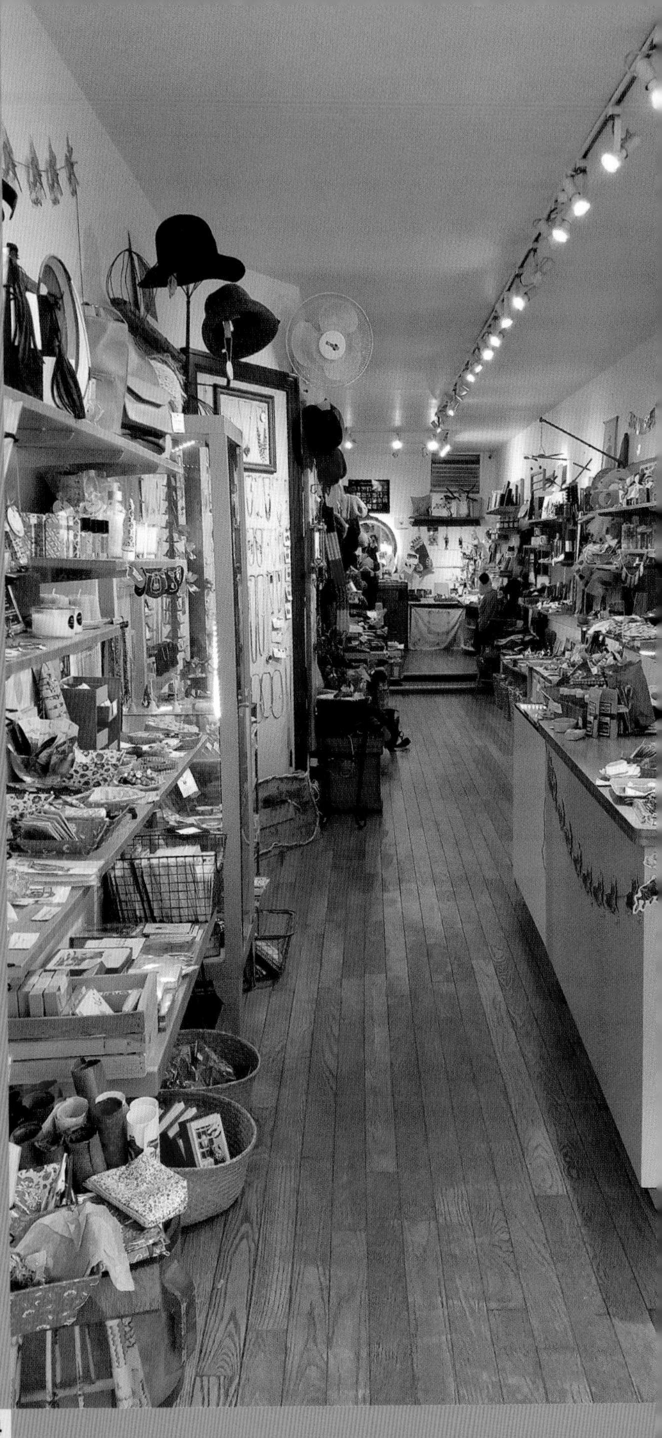

Shop

Whether you're looking for the best local products, a department store or a quirky boutique, you'll find them all in New York. In this section, shops are listed alphabetically.

SHOP

Introduction

Thought there was nothing you couldn't buy over the internet? Think again. New York is a shopping heaven, with clothing, furniture, food and souvenirs available no place else. Shopping is still one of the best ways to get an inside look at life in New York—its trends, pace, cultural influences and sense of humor. From massive department stores to small boutiques, the city has something for everyone.

One of a Kind
New York has seen a boom in artisanal and unique producers in the last decade, from chocolatiers to distilleries to jewelers. Keep an eye out for trunk shows, pop-up stores, and craft fairs where makers sell their wares.

Fashion
For fashion head for Nolita and SoHo, where small (and often expensive) boutiques line the streets. Major franchises can also be found here, along Broadway, and side streets such as Prince Street, Broome Street and Spring Street. For upscale fashion choices, head to Madison Avenue, north of 59th Street and 57th Street between 5th and Madison, where all the smartest New York shops have their outposts.

Music
Although the growth of downloads has seen the demise of many of the large music

WINDOW SHOPPING

Start on Lexington between 59th and 60th streets and you'll see the flags outside Bloomingdale's. Walk west on 57th street past Chanel, Christian Dior and Louis Vuitton and turn south on Fifth Avenue to peek into a parade of top designers such as Dolce & Gabbana, Valentino and Versace. The flagship Saks Fifth Avenue, at 50th Street, has been a bastion of high fashion since 1924.

Clockwise from top: A store on Fifth Avenue; a T-shirt that says it all; pretzels to go; looking for a bargain at

retailers, there is still much to delight the enthusiast. The city's branches of Academy Records has collections of vintage classical and rock vinyl, and used CDs; Mercer Street Books and House of Oldies are prime browsing spots in Greenwich Village; or check out the Met Opera Shop at Lincoln Center for something a little more classical. Note that most American DVDs cannot be played on European machines.

Bargains

If you're looking for a bargain, try Century 21 or visit sample sales, where designer brands are marked way down. Designer sales are often held at open showrooms over a few days. Arrive early on the first day of the sale for the best selection, though prices do drop as days go by. To find out about upcoming sales, visit thestylishcity.com/sample-sales-calendar.

A Bite to Eat

NYC is known for noshing: hot dogs, a slice of pizza, a bagel with a schmear or street food from mobile food vendors. These range from Middle Eastern falafel carts to waffle stands and spicy Korean and vegan lunch trucks. A handy guide to locating a gourmet food truck around town is roaminghunger.com.

FLEA MARKETS

You can find everything from silver and beaded jewelry to clothing, collectibles, food, artworks and antiques at the Brooklyn Flea (brooklynflea.com), on Saturday in Industry City and on Sunday in DUMBO. Uptown, check out the huge GreenFlea market in Manhattan on Sunday, 10–5.30 (✉ Columbus Avenue between 76th and 77th streets ⏲ 10–5.30). In good weather, weekend street fairs pop up in different neighborhoods. Check newyorkled.com/nyc_events_street_fairs.htm for a comprehensive list.

---

the Brooklyn Flea; don't miss the Midtown department stores; a boutique in Greenwich Village

Directory

LOWER MANHATTAN

Books
The Mysterious Bookshop
Clothes
Abercrombie & Fitch
Resurrection
Discount
Century 21
Food and Wine
The Pickle Guys
Homewares
New Kam Man

DOWNTOWN AND CHELSEA

Accessories
Village Tannery
Beauty
C.O. Bigelow
Kiehl's
Books
Barnes & Noble
Strand
Clothes
Cynthia Rowley
Hotoveli
Jeffrey New York
Kenneth Cole
Madewell
Marc Jacobs
Food and Wine
Chelsea Market
Eataly
Union Square Greenmarket
Homewares
ABC Carpet and Home
Flying Tiger Copenhagen
Shoes
DSW
Toys
Kidding Around

MIDTOWN

Clothes
Brooks Brothers
Dolce & Gabbana
Nordstrom
Thomas Pink
Department Stores
Bergdorf Goodman
Macy's
Saks Fifth Avenue
Shoes
Manolo Blahnik
Sports Goods
Niketown New York
Technology
Apple Store

UPPER EAST SIDE AND CENTRAL PARK

Books
Kitchen Arts and Letters
Clothes
Calvin Klein
Ralph Lauren
Department Stores
Bloomingdale's
Swinwear
Malia Mills

UPPER WEST SIDE

Accessories
Magpie
Beauty
Bluemercury Apothecary
Food and Wine
Zabar's
Outdoor Clothing
Patagonia

FARTHER AFIELD

Vintage Clothing
Beacon's Closet

Shopping A–Z

ABC CARPET AND HOME
abchome.com
Here are seven floors of extremely carefully edited homewares, from four-poster beds and handkerchiefs to artisanal lotions. The shared esthetic mixes mid-19th-century design museum, Venetian palace and deluxe hotel.
✚ E15 ✉ 888 Broadway/E 19th Street ☎ 212/473-3000 🚇 4, 5, 6, L, N, Q, R, W 14th Street–Union Square

ABERCROMBIE & FITCH
abercrombie.com
Teens and college grads are the core customers at this temple to slouchy American style, famous for its rather racy Bruce Weber-shot catalogs. The clothes for both men and women, though, are perfect for anyone's weekends and the prices are gentle.
✚ F21 ✉ 199 Water Street/Fulton Street ☎ 212/809-0789 (also 720 5th Avenue, tel 212/381-0110) 🚇 2, 3, 4, 5, A, C, J, Z Fulton Street–Broadway–Nassau

APPLE STORE
apple.com
This flagship store is certain to delight ingrained Mac geeks as well as those in thrall to Apple's industry-leading design. Recently doubled in size, the store is always crowded with fans. Stores can also be found in the Meatpacking District, SoHo and the Upper East and West Sides.
✚ E9 ✉ 767 5th Avenue/59th Street ☎ 212/336-1440 🚇 N, R, W 5th Avenue–59th Street

BARNES & NOBLE
barnesandnoble.com
The flagship B&N has the widest new book selection in the city. Check the website for upcoming evening readings and regular book-signing events here and at several other locations.
✚ E15 ✉ 33 E 17th Street ☎ 212/253-0810 🚇 4, 5, 6, L, N, Q, R, W 14th Street–Union Square

BEACON'S CLOSET
beaconscloset.com
This is one of the best vintage stores in Brooklyn's trendy Park Slope, with good-quality second-hand women's and men's clothing and shoes.
✚ Off map ✉ 92 5th Avenue, Brooklyn ☎ 718/230-1630 🚇 Bergen Street

The ABC Carpet and Home store

A New York institution

BERGDORF GOODMAN
bergdorfgoodman.com
For the most refined shopping experience, this eight-floor land-mark department store on the site of a Vanderbilt mansion takes the cake. The men's store is located right across the street.
🔲 E9 ✉ 754 5th Avenue/58th Street ☎ 212/753-7300 🚇 N, R, W 5th Avenue–59th Street

BLOOMINGDALE'S
bloomingdales.com
Bloomingdale's opened in 1879 and is one of the most venerable names in Manhattan, yet it keeps up with the latest trends. It's great for jewelry and handbags.
🔲 F9 ✉ Lexington/59th Street ☎ 212/705-2000 🚇 4, 5, 6, 9, F 43rd Street, 59th Street

BLUEMERCURY APOTHECARY
bluemercury.com
From top-brand cosmetics to spa treatments, hair care, fragrances and candles, Bluemercury is a welcome addition to the Upper West Side retail experience.

🔲 B5 ✉ 2305 Broadway/83rd Street ☎ 212/799-0500 🚇 1 86th Street

BROOKS BROTHERS
brooksbrothers.com
Home of preppy fashions, Brooks Brothers caters to men, women and kids with everything from classic suits to sportswear. Their basics, like boxer shorts and white dress shirts, are exceptional.
🔲 E11 ✉ 346 Madison Avenue/44th Street ☎ 212/682-8800 🚇 4, 5, 6, 7, S Grand Central

CALVIN KLEIN
calvinklein.com
The iconic New York designer's flagship store has enjoyed a recent makeover, with an Instagram-friendly deep-gold interior and floor-to-ceiling beams—an art installation in itself. Check out the homeware and vintage quilts.
🔲 E9 ✉ 654 Madison Avenue/60th Street ☎ 212/292-9000 🚇 N, R, W 5th Avenue–59th Street

CENTURY 21
c21stores.com
Practically a cult, Century 21 sells discounted chic womenswear, especially by European designers. An uptown location can be found near Lincoln Center.
🔲 E21 ✉ 22 Cortlandt Street between Church Street and Broadway ☎ 212/227-9092 🚇 4, 5 Fulton Street

CHELSEA MARKET
chelseamarket.com
More than a store, this enormous former Nabisco factory has an array of independent food bou-tiques, bakeries, cafés, coffee shops and delis under one roof. Even if you're not hungry, it's

enjoyable to stroll through for the architect-honed warehouse and to inhale the mouthwatering aromas.
➕ C15 ✉ 75 9th Avenue/15th Street ☎ 212/652-2110 🚇 A, C, E, L 14th Street

C.O. BIGELOW
bigelowchemists.com
The oldest apothecary in America (est. 1838) offers a wide range of products for pampering from head to toe. In addition to well-known international brands, the store has its own line, with everything from lotions to natural remedies.
➕ D16 ✉ 414 6th Avenue/9th Street ☎ 212/533-2700 🚇 A, B, C, D, E, F, M West 4th Street

CYNTHIA ROWLEY
cynthiarowley.com
Shop here for chic dresses, smart separates and shoes. There's also a sports and swimwear collection so, if you're in the market for one, check out the striking wetsuits.
➕ C16 ✉ 394 Bleecker Street (between Perry and West 11th streets) ☎ 212/242-3803 🚇 1 Christopher Street–Sheridan Square

DOLCE & GABBANA
dolcegabbana.com
This is the flagship New York store for luxury cutting-edge styles from fashion's dynamic duo.
➕ E9 ✉ 717 5th Avenue/55th Street ☎ 212/897-9653 🚇 N, R, W 5th Avenue E, M 5th Avenue–53rd Street

DSW
dsw.com
DSW stands for "Designer Shoe Warehouse," with Prada, Kate Spade, Via Spiga and other designer names at discounted prices. Choose from women's heels and pumps; men's loafers and sneakers; children's sandals and snowboots; handbags and more. Other branches in Midtown and the Upper West Side.
➕ E15 ✉ 40 E 14th Street, Union Square South at University Place ☎ 212/674-2146 🚇 4, 5, 6, L, N, Q, R, W Union Square

EATALY
eataly.com/nyc
Offering a cornucopia of fresh and packaged Italian foodstuffs from coffee to gelato to homemade pastas, Eataly is as close as one can come to a real Italian food bazaar. There are also a dozen places to snack or dine.
➕ D14 ✉ 200 5th Avenue/23rd Street ☎ 212/229-2560 🚇 6, R, W 23rd Street

FLYING TIGER COPENHAGEN
us.flyingtiger.com
The original US branch of this Danish chain is the go-to spot for whimsical gifts, toys and home-ware at budget prices. Selections change seasonally—and are different in the US than in Europe—so every visit is a new experience.
➕ E15 ✉ 920 Broadway/21st Street ☎ 212/777-1239 🚇 R, W 23rd Street

---

THE SHOPS AT COLUMBUS CIRCLE
The closest thing to a mall in mid-Manhattan, The Shops at Columbus Circle in the Time Warner Center has reclaimed Columbus Circle from the traffic. The stores are on the lowest four levels (restaurants above). The *pièce de résistance* is the Whole Foods Market, with a café. ➕ C9 ✉ Time Warner Center, Broadway (59th/60th streets) ☎ 212/823-6300, shopsatcolumbuscircle.com 🚇 A, B, C, D, 1 59th Street–Columbus Circle

The largest store in the world

HOTOVELI

hotoveli.com

Chic French and Italian creations dominate in this edgy West Village clothing emporium. Think neutral tones, and well-made staples.

➕ C16 ✉ 271 W 4th Street, between Perry and W 11th streets ☎ 212/206-7722 🚇 1 Christopher Street–Sheridan Square

JEFFREY NEW YORK

jeffreynewyork.com

One of the most fashionable places in the Meatpacking District, this compact designer store is the epitome of cool, with a DJ and an all-white interior. It all makes for a pleasant, but expensive, visit.

➕ B15 ✉ 449 W 14th Street/9th–10th avenues ☎ 212/206-1272 🚇 A, C, E, L 14th Street

KENNETH COLE

kennethcole.com

Don't be fooled by the minimalist design of the clothier's flagship store: If what you are looking for isn't on display, the shop's high-tech digital touchscreens showcase the full line and the store will deliver same-day in the city.

➕ F17 ✉ 328 Bowery/Bond Street ☎ 212/777-2013 🚇 6 Bleecker Street

KIDDING AROUND

kiddingaroundtoys.com

From newborns to teens, everyone will find something to their taste at this toy emporium, which stocks everything from board games to musical instruments. A branch is located in Grand Central Terminal.

➕ E15 ✉ 60 W 15th Street/Avenue of the Americas ☎ 212/645-6337 🚇 F, M 14th Street; L 6th Avenue

KIEHL'S

kiehls.com

High-end face and body products for men and women are made from naturally derived ingredients and sold in upscale black-and-white packaging. The store has been an East Village fixture since 1851—the pear tree out front commemorates one that was planted by Dutch colonial governor Peter Stuyvesant.

➕ F15 ✉ 109 3rd Avenue/13th Street ☎ 212/677-3171 🚇 L 3rd Avenue

SINGULAR SOUVENIRS

Anyone can bring home an "I Love NY" T-shirt but, for more upscale gifts, try museum gift shops. The Metropolitan Museum (▷ 44–45) and MoMA (▷ 46–47) are well stocked, the American Folk Art Museum (▷ 66) has original offerings, and the Tenement Museum (▷ 72–73) on the Lower East Side has the best selection of NYC-themed books. Prefer to eat? The Pickle Guys (▷ 124) ship across the USA. Or check out the New York City Transit Museum shop at Grand Central Terminal for unique gifts—subway token watches, anyone?

Many top designers—Dolce & Gabbana, Diane von Furstenberg, Vivienne Tam, Moschino—have sample sales where last season's merchandise is drastically discounted. Held in huge showrooms, the amenities are limited and the crowds can be daunting, but for the fashion- and budget-conscious they are a must. Check thestylishcity.com/sample-sales-calendar.

KITCHEN ARTS AND LETTERS

kitchenartsandletters.com

This independent bookstore specializing in food and drink stocks the latest bestsellers, as well as classics from chefs such as James Beard and Julia Child. The helpful staff can also source rare and out-of-print titles for you.

➕ E4 ✉ 1435 Lexington Avenue, between 93rd and 94th streets ☎ 212/876-5550 🚇 6 96th Street

MACY'S

macys.com

The sign outside says it's the largest store in the world and, by the time you've explored all 11 levels of this huge department store, you'll believe it.

➕ D12 ✉ 151 W 34th Street/Herald Square ☎ 212/695-4400 🚇 1, 2, 3, B, D, F, M, N, Q, R 34th Street

MADEWELL

madewell.com

The flagship store for this popular chain is the place to find jeans, denim and other casual classics with a chic vibe.

➕ E15 ✉ 115 5th Avenue/19th Street ☎ 212/226-6954 🚇 4, 5, 6, L, N, Q, R, W, Union Square

MAGPIE

magpienewyork.com

This charming Upper West Side boutique has everything from jewelry to baby clothes to food, all with an eco-friendly twist.

➕ B5 ✉ 488 Amsterdam Avenue/84th Street ☎ 212/579-3003 🚇 1 86th Street

MALIA MILLS

maliamills.com

This swimwear emporium sells mix-and-match pieces that are made to fit all sizes and shapes, in stylish designs. There's also a line of versatile everyday clothing.

➕ F7 ✉ 1015 Lexington Avenue/73rd Street ☎ 212/517-7485 🚇 72nd Street, 77th Street

MANOLO BLAHNIK

manoloblahnik.com

Come here for beautifully made, extravagant shoes by one of the world's great shoe designers.

➕ D10 ✉ 31 W 54th Street ☎ 212/582-3007 🚇 E, M 5th Avenue–53rd Street

MARC JACOBS

marcjacobs.com

Fashion's favorite darling, Marc Jacobs put once-Bohemian Bleecker Street on the retail map with this store.

➕ C16 ✉ 400 Bleecker Street/ W 11th Street ☎ 212/620-4021 🚇 1 Christopher Street–Sheridan Square

THE MYSTERIOUS BOOKSHOP

mysteriousbookshop.com

This is a must for mystery and crime lovers. Staff will lead you to new discoveries alongside classic writers such as Patricia Highsmith and Raymond Chandler. Rare books are available.

➕ E20 ✉ 58 Warren Street between Church Street and West Broadway ☎ 212/587-1011 Ⓜ 1, 2, 3, A, C, E Chambers Street

NEW KAM MAN

This Chinatown shop calls itself a "destination for all things Asian," and it's easy to see why. From home decor to herbal remedies, kitchenware to take-out food, there's a bit of everything here to please everyone.

➕ F19 ✉ 200 Canal Street/Mulberry Street ☎ 212/571-0330 Ⓜ 6, J, N, Q, R, W, Z Canal Street

NIKETOWN

nike.com

This lavish SoHo store has everything in sportswear, plus high-tech videos and trial zones to test equipment. Nike NYC House of Innovation 000, found at 650 Fifth Avenue, is Nike's latest and equally exciting store.

➕ E18 ✉ 529 Broadway ☎ 646/716-3740 Ⓜ 6 Spring Street; R, W Prince Street

The Mysterious Bookshop

NORDSTROM

nordstrom.com

This luxury west-coast retailer has come east with a splash, opening lavish stores for men and women. The flagship women's emporium offers seven floors of high fashion, including one level exclusively for kids. Several restaurants will fortify tired shoppers.

➕ C9 ✉ 225–235 West 57th Street/Broadway ☎ 212/295-2000; men's store 212/843-5100 Ⓜ A,B,C,D 1 59th Street-Columbus Circle

PATAGONIA

patagonia.com

If you like your outdoor wear to be environmentally conscious but still want to look good while climbing a mountain or skiing (or just looking like you might have done), this is the place for you.

➕ C6 ✉ 426 Columbus Avenue/81st Street ☎ 917/441-0011 Ⓜ B, C 81st Street–Museum of Natural History

THE PICKLE GUYS

thepickleguys.com

The Pickle Guys still brine the old-fashioned way, selling pickles, olives, pickled watermelon (in season) and more out of barrels in their small storefront, much as they might have been done a century ago.

➕ G19 ✉ 357 Grand Street/Essex Street ☎ 212/656-9739 Ⓜ F Delancey Street; J, Z Essex Street

RALPH LAUREN

ralphlauren.com

Distinguished cowboy and English country heritage looks are sold at the Rhinelander Mansion, a beautiful turn-of-the-century house.

E7 ✉ 867 Madison Avenue, between E 71st and 72nd streets ☎ 212/606-2100 🚇 6 68th Street–Hunter College

RESURRECTION

resurrectionvintage.com

You'll find a haul of pricey but perfect vintage, with an emphasis on collectible labels, including Halston, Courrèges and Ossie Clarke. The owners offer their own line of skirts and tops.

F18 ✉ 45 Great Jones Street/E Third Street ☎ 212/625-1374 🚇 6 Astor Place

SAKS FIFTH AVENUE

saksfifthavenue.com

Found on the street with the same name, this is Saks' flagship store. There's been a store here since 1924. It stocks a fabulous range of luxury designer fashions and prides itself on great service.

E10 ✉ 611 5th Avenue/49th–50th streets ☎ 212/753-4000 🚇 E, F 5th Avenue

STRAND

strandbooks.com

Filled with 18 miles (29km) of new, used and rare books, this bookstore is a New York City institution. It sells anything, from bestsellers to antique volumes. The New York City section is particularly strong.

E16 ✉ 828 Broadway/12th Street ☎ 212/473-1452 🚇 4, 5, 6, L, N, Q, R, W Union Square

THOMAS PINK

thomaspink.com

Beautifully tailored shirts for men and women line the shelves of the New York outlet of this classic British label. Quality ties, socks and belts are also available.

GREAT GREENMARKET

On four days a week (🕐 Mon, Wed, Fri, Sat 8–6) Union Square is home to the city's biggest and best greenmarket, similar to a farmers market (grownyc.org/greenmarket). It began in 1976 with just a few stands. Now, an entire culture has grown around this collection of stalls overflowing with homegrown and homemade produce from farms in the tri-state area. Favorites include maple candies, Amish cheeses and New York honey from rooftop beehives.

E10 ✉ 520 Madison Avenue/E 53rd Street ☎ 212/838-1928 🚇 E, M 5th Avenue–53rd Street

VILLAGE TANNERY

villagetannery.com

Love leather? Then look no further. Stylish leather goods, designed by artisan Sevestet, are made to order and handcrafted from the finest materials. Choose from handbags, briefcases, totes, backpacks, belts and more.

D17 ✉ 173 Bleecker Street ☎ 212/673-5444 🚇 A, B, C, D, E, F, M West 4th Street–Washington Square

ZABAR'S

zabars.com

This gourmet foodie emporium has a Jewish soul all its own and is still going strong after 80 years. Cheese, coffee, smoked fish, caviar, bread, bagels and the like are on sale downstairs, while upstairs showcases the city's best buys in kitchenwares and housewares. There's even an on-site café if you can't wait to sample the produce.

B6 ✉ 2245 Broadway/80th Street ☎ 212/787-2000 🚇 1 79th Street

Entertainment

Once you're done with sightseeing for the day, you'll find lots of other great things to do with your time in this chapter, even if all you want to do is relax with a drink. In this section, establishments are listed alphabetically.

ENTERTAINMENT

Introduction

As the sun sets over New York, the city becomes a sultry, romantic and mysterious place. For spectacular sunset views, stroll along the pedestrian path on the banks of the Hudson River on the West Side, then wander through Times Square as the bright billboards pop out from the dark sky.

Nightlife

As New Yorkers explore new frontiers in the city, the Meatpacking District—once known for drugs and prostitution—has become home to bars and clubs. You never know who might show at the chic Top of the Standard (848 Washington Street, tel 212/645-7600) and TAO Downtown (92 9th Avenue at 16th Street, tel 212/888-2724). At the other end of the spectrum are neighborhood joints such as the Ear Inn (326 Spring Street at Washington Street, tel 212/226-9060) and Fat Cat (75 Christopher Street in West Village, tel 212/675-6056)—friendly dives where the beer flows and the music is loud.

A short stroll away, a string of music bars sit cheek by jowl along two blocks of Bleecker Street between LaGuardia Place and Sullivan Street, including the classic folk-rock haven The Bitter End (147 Bleecker Street, tel 212/673-7030), still going strong after more than 50 years. Around the corner is Café Wha? (▷ 132), where Dylan and Hendrix once played, and now a nightclub.

FOR A LAUGH

Comedy clubs are a great way to sample New York's sense of humor. Try venues such as Caroline's on Broadway (✉ 1626 Broadway, at 50th Street ☎ 212/757-4100, carolines.com), Upright Citizens Brigade Theatre (✉ 555 W 42nd Street/11th Avenue ☎ 212/366-9176; ucbtheatre.com), Comic Strip Live (✉ 1568 2nd Avenue ☎ 212/861-9386). Stand Up NY (▷ 137) and Gotham (▷ 134) are also popular.

Clockwise from top: Blue Note in Greenwich Village is one of the best places for jazz; the old Paramount Theater, Times Square; Alice Tully Hall, Lincoln Center;

Another hot nightlife neighborhood is the Lower East Side, where there's a multitude of bars fanning out from Ludlow and Stanton streets. Leading the pack are Arlene's Grocery (▷ 131), Pianos (158 Ludlow Street, tel 212/505-3733) and Rockwood Music Hall (196 Allen Street, tel 212/477-4155).

Broadway and Beyond
Top Broadway shows can be expensive, but you can pick up some great bargains at the TKTS booth in Times Square and other locations (tdf.org/tkts). Off-Broadway venues are less expensive and you might catch the next big hit on its way up. A night at Lincoln Center (▷ 42–43) is an unforgettable New York experience, whether you opt for a production at the Metropolitan Opera (▷ 135), a symphony at David Geffen Hall (▷ 133), a ballet at the David H. Koch Theater (▷ 133), or one of the more intimate venues.

Take to the Water
Circle Line Cruises' evening boat rides around Manhattan are a relaxing and memorable way to experience the world's most famous skyline. Board at Pier 83, at 42nd Street on the Hudson River or Pier 16, South Street Seaport (tel 212/563-3200). Tour guides on board relate the legends of the city (circleline.com).

LIVE MUSIC

Rock bands perform at Bowery Ballroom (✉ 6 Delancey Street ☎ 212/260-4700, boweryballroom.com) and Irving Plaza (✉ 17 Irving Plaza ☎ 212/777-6800, irving-plaza.com). Madison Square Garden (▷ 135) hosts blockbuster tours. There's everything from classical music to pop at Carnegie Hall (▷ 132). Among the top jazz clubs are Blue Note (▷ 132) and Village Vanguard (✉ 178 7th Avenue South ☎ 212/255-4037, villagevanguard.com) in Greenwich Village, and Iridium in Midtown (✉ 1650 Broadway ☎ 212/582-2121, theiridium.com).

Gotham Comedy Club; a quiet table for two in the Meatpacking District; take to the water to see the New York skyline by night

Directory

LOWER MANHATTAN
Bars
The Dead Rabbit Grocery and Grog
Parkside Lounge
The Porterhouse at Fraunces Tavern
Cinema
Film Forum
Clubs
Arlene's Grocery
SOB's
Comedy
Comedy Cellar
Live Music
City Winery

DOWNTOWN AND CHELSEA
Bars
McSorley's Old Ale House
Pete's Tavern
White Horse Tavern
Cabaret
Joe's Pub
Comedy
Gotham Comedy Club
Jazz
Blue Note
Live Music
Café Wha?
Mercury Lounge
Theater/Performance
Cherry Lane Theatre
Joyce Theater

MIDTOWN
Bars
Four Seasons Hotel TY Bar
Classical Music
Carnegie Hall
Jazz
Birdland
Live Music
Madison Square Garden
PlayStation Theater
Theater/Performance
The New Victory Theater
New World Stages

Radio City Music Hall
Roundabout Theater Company
Signature Theatre

UPPER EAST SIDE AND CENTRAL PARK
Bars
Auction House
Comedy
Dangerfield's
Jazz
Café Carlyle
Literary Events/Readings
92nd Street Y
Theater/Performance
Florence Gould Hall
Shakespeare in the Park

UPPER WEST SIDE
Bars
Ascent
Classical Music
Cathedral of St. John the Divine
David Geffen Hall
Metropolitan Opera
Comedy
Stand Up NY
Dance
David H. Koch Theater
Jazz
Dizzy's Club Coca Cola
Smoke
Live Music
Beacon Theatre
Theater/Performance
Symphony Space

FARTHER AFIELD
Bars
Barbès
Union Hall
Live Music
Brooklyn Steel

Entertainment A–Z

92ND STREET Y

92Y.org

A varied program of events is held here, including readings by renowned authors, folk music, jazz and lectures on a range of subjects.

🞖 E4 ✉ 1395 Lexington Avenue/92nd Street ☎ 212/415-5500 🚇 6 96th Street

ARLENE'S GROCERY

arlenesgrocery.net

This is one of the best live music clubs in the city. Arlene's prides itself on helping new bands.

🞖 G18 ✉ 95 Stanton Street, between Ludlow and Orchard streets ☎ 212/358-1633 🚇 F, M 2nd Avenue

ASCENT

ascentloungenyc.com

Enjoy impressively designed surroundings, fine food and drink, and stunning views of Central Park and Broadway at this elegant bar.

🞖 C9 ✉ Time Warner Center, Columbus Circle ☎ 212/823-9770 🚇 A, B, C, D 59th Street–Columbus Circle

AUCTION HOUSE

theauctionhousenyc.com

With sumptuous red velvet drapes, a fireplace, sofas and candlelight, this is more suited to a romantic drink than a rowdy night out on the town. The no-furs, no-sneakers dress code gives an idea of the casual-chic ambience.

🞖 F4 ✉ 300 E 89th Street/2nd Avenue ☎ 212/427-4458 🚇 Q 86th Street

Check out the cocktails

BARBÈS

barbesbrooklyn.com

This Brooklyn bar and live music venue is named for a neighborhood in Paris known for its North African community. In its intimate performance space at the back, Barbès stages an eclectic music program, from Slavic soul to Afrobeat and Cuban jazz.

🞖 Off map ✉ 376 9th Street ☎ 347/422-0248 🚇 F 7th Avenue

BEACON THEATRE

beacontheatre.com

The Beacon is one of the premier venues in the city, featuring multi-night stands by legendary artists such as Bob Dylan and Ringo Starr, as well as many rising stars.

🞖 B7 ✉ 2124 Broadway/74th Street ☎ 212/465-6000 🚇 1, 2, 3 72nd Street

---

ROOFTOP BARS

Toast the brilliant lights of the city in these lofty lairs: Dear Irving on Hudson, at the Aliz Hotel Times Square (✉ 310 West 40th Street/8th-9th Avenues ☎ 917/261-6908); 230 Fifth (230 Fifth Avenue/27th Street ☎ 212/725-4300); Skylight Lounge, Watson Hotel (✉ 440 West 57th Street/9th-10th Avenues ☎ 212/634-6116); Roof at Park South, Park South Hotel (✉ 125 East 27th Street/Park-Lexington ☎ 212/204-5227).

Carnegie Hall

BIRDLAND

birdlandjazz.com

Big names, big bands, John Coltrane tributes and Cuban music are the rage here. The club was established here in 1949.

🚰 C11 ✉ 315 W 44th Street/8th–9th avenues ☎ 212/581-3080 🚇 A, C, E 42nd Street–Port Authority Bus Terminal

BLUE NOTE

bluenote.net

Jazz artists play two shows nightly at this popular Village club and restaurant. The Sunday brunch deal of food and a show is great value.

🚰 D17 ✉ 131 W 3rd Street/6th Avenue–MacDougal Street ☎ 212/475-8592 🚇 A, B, C, D, E, F, M 4th Street–Washington Square

BROOKLYN STEEL

bowerypresents.com

This music venue in Williamsburg is a huge, down-to-earth, 1,800-capacity space, favoring indie-rock bands, as well as major DJ sets.

🚰 Off map ✉ 319 Frost Street ☎ 888/929-7849 🚇 L Graham Avenue

CAFÉ CARLYLE

thecarlyle.com

This lounge in the Carlyle Hotel is home to smooth singers and jazz bands. Look in at Bemelmans Bar, with its murals of Central Park by Ludwig Bemelmans.

🚰 E6 ✉ 35 E 76th Street, Madison Avenue ☎ 212/744-1600 🚇 6 77th Street

CAFÉ WHA?

cafewha.com

In business since the 1950s, this has been a hot spot ever since Bob Dylan and Jimi Hendrix used to hang out here. Bruce Springsteen started his career here. It's still going strong, with bands performing nightly and styles ranging from R&B to soul, modern rock and indie pop.

🚰 D17 ✉ 115 MacDougal Street/Minetta Lane ☎ 212/254-3706 🚇 A, B, C, D, E, F, M 4th Street–Washington Square

CARNEGIE HALL

carnegiehall.org

This world-class venue, which houses three recital halls, features an eclectic program from classical artists to folk singers, world music and pop. With so much choice, there's something for everyone.

🚰 D9 ✉ 881 7th Avenue/57th Street ☎ 212/247-7800 🚇 N, Q, R, W 57th Street; E 7th Avenue

CATHEDRAL OF ST. JOHN THE DIVINE

stjohndivine.org

The cathedral provides a varied program of liturgical, cultural and civic events including choral, classical and poetry recitals.

🚰 B1 ✉ 1047 Amsterdam Avenue/112th Street ☎ 212/316-7540 🚇 1 Cathedral Parkway–110th Street

CHERRY LANE THEATRE

cherrylanetheatre.org

This historic theater in Greenwich Village presents a vibrant program of landmark plays and works by emerging playwrights.

✚ C17 ✉ 38 Commerce Street between Barrow and Bedford streets ☎ 212/989-2020 🚇 1 Christopher Street–Sheridan Square

CITY WINERY

citywinery.com/newyork

Events at the City Winery range from intimate evenings with singer-songwriters to gourmet cooking demonstrations. It's also a fully functioning winery, with tastings and a shop.

✚ D18 ✉ 155 Varick Street/Vandam Street ☎ 212/608-0555 🚇 C, E Spring Street; 1 Houston

COMEDY CELLAR

comedycellar.com

A cozy Greenwich Village spot, this attracts well-known comedians from time to time. The intimate nature of the venue means you are quite likely to find you are part of the show, so be warned.

✚ D17 ✉ 117 MacDougal Street, between W 3rd Street and Minetta Lane, and 130 W 3rd Street ☎ 212/254-3480 🚇 A, B, C, D, E, F, M 4th Street–Washington Square

DANGERFIELD'S

dangerfields.com

This basement comedy club, established in 1969, is still going strong and claims to be the oldest in the world. Those that have performed on its tiny stage include Jay Leno and Jim Carrey.

✚ F9 ✉ 1118 1st Avenue/61st Street ☎ 212/593-1650 🚇 4, 5, 6 59th Street

DAVID GEFFEN HALL

lincolncenter.org

In 2015, David Geffen donated $100 million to rename and revamp the Avery Fisher Hall concert venue. It's home to the New York Philharmonic, but touring artists and orchestras also come to perform here.

✚ B8 ✉ 10 Lincoln Center Plaza, Columbus Avenue/65th Street ☎ 212/721-6500 🚇 1 66th Street–Lincoln Center

DAVID H. KOCH THEATER

davidhkochtheater.com

nycballet.com

The sumptuous home of the New York City Ballet, which performs here September through June.

✚ B8 ✉ 20 Lincoln Center Plaza at 63rd Street ☎ 212/496-0600 🚇 1 66th Street–Lincoln Center

THE DEAD RABBIT GROCERY AND GROG

deadrabbitnyc.com

Every drink on the Dead Rabbit's extensive upstairs menu is historically sourced, giving patrons a flavor of old New York.

✚ E23 ✉ 30 Water Street/Broad Street ☎ 646/422-7906 🚇 1 South Ferry; R, W Whitehall

DIZZY'S CLUB COCA COLA
jazz.org/dizzys
Jazz at this intimate club is—in the spirit of Dizzy Gillespie—designed to ensure that performers and spectators alike relaaaaax. There are late-night sessions Tuesday through Saturday.
C9 ⊠ Time Warner Center at Broadway/60th Street, 5th floor ☎ 212/258-9595 🚇 1, A, B, C, D 59th Street–Columbus Circle

FILM FORUM
filmforum.org
New York's best revival house shows everything from silent films (with live accompaniment) to independent movie premieres, documentaries and classics.
D18 ⊠ 209 W Houston Street/Varick Street ☎ 212/727-8110 🚇 1 Houston Street

FLORENCE GOULD HALL
fiaf.org
Associated with the Alliance Française, this concert hall stages music, dance, jazz and readings with a French theme.
E9 ⊠ 55 E 59th Street/Park–Madison avenues ☎ 212/355-6160 🚇 N, R, W 5th Avenue–59th Street

FOUR SEASONS HOTEL TY BAR
fourseasons.com/newyork
An I.M. Pei design, a smooth vibe and a great Martini menu make the TY lobby bar an excellent choice for cocktails.
E9 ⊠ 57 E 57th Street/Madison Avenue ☎ 212/758-5700 🚇 4, 5, 6 Lexington Avenue–59th Street

GOTHAM COMEDY CLUB
gothamcomedyclub.com
Gotham showcases top stars (including the likes of Jerry Seinfeld, Larry David and Dave Chappelle), as well as up-and-coming comedians.
C14 ⊠ 208 W 23rd Street/7th Avenue ☎ 212/367-9000 🚇 1 23rd Street; F, Path 23rd Street

JOE'S PUB
joespub.publictheater.org
Known for its sound quality, Joe's always has an interesting, varied line-up of singers, comedians, magicians and burlesque artists.
E16 ⊠ The Public Theater, 425 Lafayette Street/Astor Place ☎ 212/539-8778 🚇 R, W 8th Street–NYU; 6 Astor Place

JOYCE THEATER
joyce.org
From Cuba to India and Monte Carlo to Argentina, leading modern dance companies from the US and around the world perform at this art-deco gem, a 1941 movie theater converted in 1982 into an intimate dance venue. Check schedules as programs change almost weekly.

CABARET
The term has undergone so many image overhauls, it's now settled into being a catch-all for entertainment options ranging from off-Broadway cabaret theater and downtown crooners sitting around the piano bar at Duplex (⊠ 61 Christopher Street ☎ 212/255-5438, theduplex.com) to the Broadway supper club at 54 Below (⊠ 254 W 54th Street ☎ 646/476-3551, 54below.com). Joe's Pub (above) is among the venues that offer what you might call classic, though modernized, cabaret.

New York's late-night scene ranges from all-night parties to more staid amusements. The Meatpacking District is home to many popular spots, including sister clubs Le Bain (🏠 444 W 13th Street ☎ 212/645-7600), with its rooftop hot tubs, and Top of the Standard (🏠 848 Washington Street), atop the High Line. At the IFC Center (🏠 323 6th Avenue/ W 3rd Street ☎ 212/924-7771), scary weekend Midnight Movies have a loyal following.

🏠 C15 ✉ 175 Eighth Avenue/19th Street ☎ 212/691-9740 🚇 C 23rd Street, A 14th Street

MADISON SQUARE GARDEN

msg.com

The giant concrete circle, often called MSG, is one of the city's major venues for music and sporting events. For the box office, enter the Main Ticket Lobby at 7th Avenue and 32nd Street.
🏠 C13 ✉ 4 Pennsylvania Plaza ☎ 212/465-6741 🚇 1, 2, 3, A, C, E 34th Street–Penn Station

MCSORLEY'S OLD ALE HOUSE

mcsorleysoldalehouse.nyc

New York's oldest remaining saloon (1854) served Abe Lincoln and John Lennon, and still draws a crowd with its sawdust-covered floors and coal-burning stove.
🏠 F16 ✉ 15 E 7th Street/3rd Avenue ☎ 212/473-9148 🚇 6 Astor Place

MERCURY LOUNGE

mercuryloungenyc.com

Its laid-back atmosphere attracts eclectic performers and tickets are very reasonable. The Strokes famously got their start here.
🏠 F17 ✉ 217 E Houston Street/Essex Street ☎ 212/260-4700 🚇 F 2nd Avenue

METROPOLITAN OPERA

metopera.org

The gala openings at this world-class opera house rank among the most glamorous of the city's events. Visit the website at noon for same-day rush tickets. The season runs from October to April.
🏠 B8 ✉ 30 Lincoln Center ☎ 212/362-6000 🚇 1 66th Street–Lincoln Center

THE NEW VICTORY THEATER

newvictory.org

If you have kids who are six and over, there's bound to be something here to thrill them and keep them entertained.
🏠 C11 ✉ 209 W 42nd Street/7th–8th avenues ☎ 646/223-3010 🚇 1, 2, 3, 7, N, Q, R, S, W Times Square–42nd Street

NEW WORLD STAGES

newworldstages.com

Check out the top off-Broadway productions, from musicals to kids' shows, at this state-of-the-art theatrical venue.
🏠 C10 ✉ 340 W 50th Street/8th Avenue ☎ 646/871-1730 🚇 C, E 50th Street

SUMMER IN THE CITY

One of the best reasons to brave the summer heat in New York is the wonderful choice of free entertainment put on by many of the city's premier cultural institutions. Without paying a dime it's possible to enjoy alfresco operas, theater, art, eating, jazz, classical music, movies, dance, rock-and-roll, blues and folk music. Many people arrive early for park performances by popular artists and stake out a good spot for a picnic.

ENTERTAINMENT

PARKSIDE LOUNGE

parksidelounge.net

Parkside hosts live music, stand-up and karaoke, as well as those just having a beer. It's great for night owls as it's open until 4am.

➕ G17 ✉ 317 E Houston Street/Attorney Street ☎ 212/673-6270 Ⓜ F, M 2nd Avenue

PETE'S TAVERN

petestavern.com

A favorite with locals, this fine 150-year-old Gramercy Park saloon has a welcoming feel. The happy hour (Mon–Fri 4–7) serves free hors d'oeuvres.

➕ E15 ✉ 129 E 18th Street/Irving Place ☎ 212/473-7676 Ⓜ 4, 5, 6, L, N, Q, R, W 14th Street–Union Square

PLAYSTATION THEATER

playstationtheater.com

This theater is a medium-size venue for decent music acts in a great location in Times Square.

➕ C11/D11 ✉ 1515 Broadway/44th Street ☎ 212/930-1950 Ⓜ 1, 2, 3, 7, N, Q, R, S, W Times Square–42nd Street

THE PORTERHOUSE AT FRAUNCES TAVERN

fraucestavern.com

This 18th-century watering hole is the first US branch of Dublin's Porterhouse Brewing Company. It has fine ales, live music and DJs.

➕ E22 ✉ 54 Pearl Street/Broad Street ☎ 212/968-1776 Ⓜ R, W Whitehall Street

RADIO CITY MUSIC HALL

radiocity.com

This landmark art-deco theater hosts major music and family shows. The holiday show is a city tradition. One-hour tours offered.

➕ D10 ✉ 1260 6th Avenue/50th Street ☎ 212/247-4777 Ⓞ Varied; tours daily 9.30–5 Ⓜ B, D, F, M 40th–50th streets–Rockefeller Center

ROUNDABOUT THEATRE COMPANY

roundabouttheatre.org

This non-profit is one of the city's major companies. Three theaters on and off Broadway present both new work and revivals, often with top stars.

➕ D11 ✉ American Airlines Theater, 227 West 42nd Street (between 7th–8th Avenues), at two other locations ☎ 212-719-1300 Ⓜ 1, 2, 3, 7, N, R, W, Q, S Times Square

SHAKESPEARE IN THE PARK

publictheater.org

The Shakespeare festival is a real highlight of summer in Central Park and has been running for more than 60 years. Line up for free tickets from noon on performance days.

C6 ✉ Delacorte Theater in Central Park, 81st Street (west side) ☎ 212/539-8500 🚇 B, C 81st Street

SIGNATURE THEATRE
signaturetheatre.org
Every season at this off-Broadway house, designed by Frank Gehry, has a new playwright-in-residence from the first ranks of American theater. Even without tickets, you can enjoy the café/bar.

B11 ✉ 480 W 42nd Street/10th Avenue ☎ 212/244-7529 🚇 A, C, E 42nd Street

SMOKE
smokejazz.com
This intimate jazz lounge hosts both local and well-known names. The fixed-price dinners are good value, as is the Sunday brunch.

B2 ✉ 2751 Broadway/106th Street ☎ 212/864-6662 🚇 1 103rd Street

SOB'S
sobs.com
The Latin rhythms played here will keep you dancing at the tropically themed club, Sounds of Brazil. Hear African, reggae and other island music.

D18 ✉ 204 Varick Street/Houston Street ☎ 212/243-4940 🚇 1 Houston Street

STAND UP NY
standupny.com
Aspiring comics try out their new routines in this traditional comedy club that has also hosted the likes of Jerry Seinfeld, Chris Rock and Jon Stewart.

B6 ✉ 236 W 78th Street/Broadway ☎ 212/595-0850 🚇 1 79th Street

SYMPHONY SPACE
symphonyspace.org
Head here for music, storytelling, readings, children's theater, dance, film, comedy and more. There's often more than one event a day.

B4 ✉ 2537 Broadway/95th Street ☎ 212/864-5400 🚇 1, 2, 3 96th Street

UNION HALL
unionhallny.com
This casual lounge-bar/restaurant in Brooklyn's Park Slope has two popular *bocce* lanes (like indoor bowls), outdoor seating and a stage for live music and comedy.

Off map ✉ 702 Union Street/5th Avenue ☎ 718/638-4400 🚇 Union Street

WHITE HORSE TAVERN
whitehorsetavern1880.com
This sprawling 1880s bar has been popular with writers and artists over the years, and was the last watering hole of Welsh poet Dylan Thomas. It serves bar food, including weekend brunch.

C16 ✉ 567 Hudson Street/11th Street ☎ 212/989-3956 🚇 1 Christopher Street–Sheridan Square

Radio City, famous since the 1930s

Eat

There are places to eat across the city to suit all tastes and budgets. In this section, establishments are listed alphabetically.

EAT

Introduction

In this global melting pot, you can find just about every world cuisine from African to Vietnamese in settings from budget hole-in-the wall to haute cuisine palaces.

New Takes on Tradition

New York also has its own dining traditions for visitors to share, with dishes like New York strip steaks and Manhattan clam chowder. But other favorites change with the times. Brunch is still the classic weekend ritual in Greenwich Village and SoHo, but healthier veggie choices are now in the mix (▷ 144). As the legendary New York delis are disappearing, updated versions like Russ and Daughters Café are taking their place (127 Orchard Street/Delancey-Rivington, tel 212-475-4880). Food halls with many choices are multiplying (▷ 142). Pizza by the slice remains a city standby. To sample the traditional thin-crusted New York pizza baked in a coal-fired, brick-oven, visit pioneers like Grimaldi's, in Brooklyn (▷ 145), or John's, 302 E 12th Street (tel 212/475-9531).

Fine Dining

You can enjoy world-class dining in New York, at places like Per Se (▷ 148), Le Bernardin (▷ 142) or Eleven Madison Park (▷ 144), but reserve well in advance. Top restaurants have top prices, $200 or more per person, including tax and tip.

TAXES, TIPPING AND FINANCIAL MATTERS

A sales tax of 8.875 percent will be added to your dining bill. The minimum tip (with good service) is 15 percent; people often double the tax for a 17.75 percent tip. Many restaurants offer fixed-price menus, which are good value. Watch for New York Restaurant Week, held twice a year in winter and summer. This special promotion offers a three-course menu at reduced rates for lunch and dinner at many restaurants; this deal is often extended so it's always worth checking if it's available.

From top: Pancakes with maple syrup in a New York diner; John's Pizzeria; Café Boulud, a top restaurant; cheeseburger with fries

EAT

Directory

LOWER MANHATTAN
Asian
Mission Chinese Food
Oriental Garden
Casual
The Bailey
Bubby's
Delicatessen
Classic NY
Katz's Deli
The Odeon
Fine Dining
Delmonico's
Manhatta

DOWNTOWN AND CHELSEA
American
Union Square Café
Asian
Momofuku Ssäm Bar
Pondicheri
Contemporary
North Square
Fine Dining
Del Posto
Eleven Madison Park
Gotham Bar and Grill
Ukrainian
Veselka

MIDTOWN
Asian
Kajitsu
Nobu Fifty Seven
Casual
Forty Carrots
Grand Central Terminal Dining
    Concourse (▷ panel, 145)
John's Pizzeria
Classic NY
'21' Club
Oyster Bar
Sarge's Deli

Fine Dining
Le Bernardin
Casa Lever
Per Se
Greek
Uncle Nick's

UPPER EAST SIDE AND CENTRAL PARK
Casual
Jackson Hole
Classic NY
The Loeb Boathouse
Fine Dining
Daniel
French
Café Boulud
Middle Eastern
A La Turka
Persepolis

UPPER WEST SIDE
Casual
Barney Greengrass
Boat Basin Café
Fine Dining
Jean-Georges
Italian
Carmine's
Mexican
Rosa Mexicano
Vegetarian
Blossom on Columbus

FARTHER AFIELD
Casual
Grimaldi's
Classic NY
Peter Luger Steak House
Contemporary
Blue Ribbon Brasserie
Henry's End
Fine Dining
River Café

EAT

Eating A–Z

PRICES

Prices are approximate, based on a 3-course meal for one person.

$$$	over $60
$$	$40–$60
$	under $40

'21' CLUB $$$

21club.com

With a history spanning more than eight decades, this popular eatery doffs a cap to its speakeasy days. Choose from the fixed-price menus or an extensive à la carte featuring lobster, steak, salmon, seasonal produce and much more. The eponymous '21' burger is a perennial favorite.

➕ D10 ✉ 21 W 52nd Street/5th–6th avenues ☎ 212/582-7200 ◷ Mon–Fri lunch, Mon–Sat dinner 🚇 B, D, F, M 47th–50th streets–Rockefeller Center

A LA TURKA $$

alaturkany.com

A sociable neighborhood favorite for over 20 years, A La Turka's menu features grilled meats and fish, a dozen kinds of kebabs and a terrific chopped shepherd's salad. Try the *lahmecon*, traditional Turkish pizza. There's music and belly dancing on Thursdays.

➕ F7 ✉ 1417 2nd Avenue/74th Street ☎ 212/744-2424 ◷ Daily lunch and dinner 🚇 6 77th Street

THE BAILEY $$

thebaileynyc.com

Just off Wall Street, this is a big hit with the Financial District crowd. The offerings include pub favorites like fish and chips and shepherd's pie, plus a wide American menu and a selection of salads. At the busy bar you can order snacks, burgers or mac 'n' cheese while watching sports on TV.

➕ E22 ✉ 52 William Street ☎ 212/859-2200 ◷ Daily breakfast, lunch and dinner, weekend brunch 🚇 2, 3, 4, 5 Wall Street

BARNEY GREENGRASS $–$$

barneygreengrass.com

An Upper West Side tradition since 1929, this is frantic on weekends, when locals feast on huge platters of smoked fish—whitefish, sablefish, sturgeon and lox—or have the same ingredients packed into a hearty sandwich.

➕ B5 ✉ 541 Amsterdam Avenue/86th Street ☎ 212/724-4707 ◷ Tue–Fri 8.30–4, Sat–Sun 8.30–5 🚇 1 86th Street

LE BERNARDIN $$$

le-bernardin.com

Frenchman Eric Ripert is known to be the fish maestro. Exquisite, inventive dishes are served by super-attentive waiters.

➕ D10 ✉ 155 W 51st Street/7th Avenue ☎ 212/554-1515 ◷ Mon–Fri lunch, Mon–Sat dinner 🚇 B, D, F, M 47th–50th streets–Rockefeller Center

FOOD HALLS

Curated, gourmet food halls are very popular, where diners can select from different cuisines. In addition to Eataly (▷ 121), check out the Pennsy at Penn Station (✉ 2 Pennsylvania Plaza ☎ 917/475-1830), Grand Central Terminal (▷ 145), The Todd English Food Hall in the lower level of the Plaza Hotel (✉ 1 West 59th Street ☎ 212/986-9260) and Urbanspace Vanderbilt, outside Grand Central (✉ Corner of Vanderbilt Avenue/45th Street ☎ 646/747-0822), home to a constantly changing line-up of concept outlets.

BLOSSOM ON COLUMBUS $$

blossomnyc.com

This cozy branch of the Blossom empire boasts a selection of bio-dynamic beers and wines, and top vegan fare. The soy bacon cheeseburger has a devoted following.
➕ C5 ✉ 507 Columbus Avenue/84th Street ☎ 212/875-2600 ⏰ Daily lunch and dinner, weekend brunch 🚇 B, C 81st Street–Museum of Natural History

BLUE RIBBON BRASSERIE $$

blueribbonrestaurants.com

There's a Manhattan feel to this huge modern-American favorite in Brooklyn's Park Slope—not surprising, since it also has a SoHo outlet (97 Sullivan Street/Prince Street), liked by off-duty chefs. It combines creativity with comfort food.
➕ Off map ✉ 280 5th Avenue/ 1st Street, Brooklyn ☎ 718/840-0404 ⏰ Daily dinner 🚇 R Union Street

BOAT BASIN CAFÉ $

boatbasincafe.com

It's hard to find this open-air café serving burgers, salads and sandwiches on the banks of the

Bubby's in Tribeca

Hudson but, if you do, enjoy dazzling views from the terrace.
➕ A6 ✉ W 79th Street/Hudson River ☎ 212/496-5542 ⏰ Late Mar–Oct (weather permitting) daily lunch and dinner 🚇 1 79th Street

BUBBY'S $

bubbys.com

A Tribeca favorite serving Bubby's all-American BLTs, chicken clubs, meat loaf and fries, and pies, including Key lime and banoffee. Expect a wait for the popular weekend brunch.
➕ D19 ✉ 120 Hudson Street ☎ 212/219-0666 ⏰ Daily 8am–11pm 🚇 1, 9 Franklin Street; A, C, E Canal Street

CAFÉ BOULUD $$–$$$

cafeboulud.com

Daniel Boulud's French restaurant has classical, seasonal and ethnic influences. The prix-fixe lunches are good value and live jazz is featured on Friday nights.
➕ E6 ✉ 20 E 76th Street/5th–Madison avenues ☎ 212/772-2600 ⏰ Daily breakfast, lunch, dinner, Sun brunch 🚇 6 77th Street

CARMINE'S $$

carminesnyc.com

This beloved, raucous place serves Sicilian-Italian dishes family-style—on huge platters to share. It's not for picky foodies, but it's fun.
➕ B4 ✉ 2450 Broadway/90th Street ☎ 212/362-2200 ⏰ Daily lunch and dinner 🚇 1, 2, 3 96th Street–Broadway

CASA LEVER $$$

casalever.com

The ocean-liner-esque design is the star at this restaurant, downstairs in the Lever House building, but it's worth a visit just for the chef's contemporary twists on northern Italian classics.

➕ E10 ✉ 390 Park Avenue/53rd Street ☎ 212/888-2700 🕐 Mon–Fri breakfast, lunch and dinner, Sat dinner 🚇 6 51st Street; E, M Lexington Avenue–53rd Street

DANIEL $$$

danielnyc.com

This formal restaurant serves modern French dishes—opt for the seven-course tasting menu to fully appreciate chef Daniel Boulud's brilliance. Dessert arrives with its own basket of warm madeleines.

➕ E8 ✉ 60 E 65th Street/Madison–Park avenues ☎ 212/288-0033 🕐 Mon–Sat dinner 🚇 6 68th Street–Hunter College

DEL POSTO $$$

delposto.com

Noted restaurateurs Joe and Lidia Bastianich created this swanky, deco-looking, big-night-out Italian restaurant, complete with piano player and tableside preparations.

➕ B15 ✉ 85 10th Avenue/16th Street ☎ 212/497-8090 🕐 Mon–Fri lunch and dinner, Sat–Sun dinner 🚇 A, C, E, L 14th Street

DELICATESSEN $

delicatessennyc.com

In need of some comfort food? At this Nolita restaurant you can start with cheeseburger spring rolls, followed by steak-frites.

➕ F18 ✉ 54 Prince Street/Lafayette Street ☎ 212/226-0211 🕐 Mon–Fri breakfast, lunch and dinner, Sat–Sun brunch and dinner 🚇 N, R Prince Street

DELMONICO'S $$$

delmoniconsy.com

Old New York lives on at this pioneer restaurant founded in 1867, renovated but still with its old-world charm and serving excellent steaks.

➕ F22 ✉ 56 Beaver Street/William Street ☎ 212/509-1144 🕐 Lunch Mon–Fri, dinner Mon–Sat 🚇 2, 3 Wall Street; 4, 5 Bowling Green; J, Z Broad Street

ELEVEN MADISON PARK $$$

elevenmadisonpark.com

This is one of the best restaurants in New York. Chef Daniel Humm delivers knockout tasting menus of his contemporary American cuisine at stratospheric prices. Reserve well in advance, or get a sample for less at the bar.

➕ E14 ✉ 11 Madison Avenue/24th Street ☎ 212/889-0905 🕐 Daily dinner, Fri–Sun lunch 🚇 6, R, W 23rd Street

FORTY CARROTS $

bloomingdales.com/59th-street

Take a break at this hideaway on the 7th floor of Bloomingdales. The freshly made sandwiches, salads and soups are tasty and the frozen yogurt is the best in town.

➕ F9 ✉ Bloomingdales, 1000 3rd Avenue/59th–60th Streets ☎ 212/705-3085 🕐 Daily lunch and dinner to 7.30pm 🚇 4, 5, 6 59th Street

---

VEGGIE DELIGHTS

With a third of Americans now opting to eat vegetarian at least once a week, New York has become a center for creative meat-free restaurants. At the higher end are Kajitsu (▷ 146) and Blossom on Columbus (▷ 143). Veggie lovers should also seek out Peacefood Café (✉ 460 Amsterdam Avenue/82nd Street ☎ 212/362-2266) and celebrity chef Chloe Coscarelli's By Chloe (✉ 185 Bleecker Street/MacDougal Street ☎ 212/290-8000).

EAT

GOTHAM BAR AND GRILL $$$

gothambarandgrill.com

This light and airy restaurant epitomizes New York grandeur, with world-class dishes such as miso-marinated black cod. The greenmarket lunch is good value.

🔲 E16 ✉ 12 E 12th Street/5th Avenue ☎ 212/620-4020 🕐 Mon–Fri lunch and dinner, Sat–Sun dinner only 🚇 4, 5, 6, L, N, Q, R, W 14th Street–Union Square

GRIMALDI'S $

grimaldis-pizza.com

Grimaldi's dates back to 1905. Pick a basic pizza or add your own toppings for a mouthwatering masterpiece. Constant lines are testament to its reputation. Credit cards are not accepted here.

🔲 H21 ✉ 1 Front Street (under Brooklyn Bridge) ☎ 718/858-4300 🕐 Daily lunch, dinner 🚇 2, 3 Clark Street: A, C High Street

HENRY'S END $$

henrysend.com

This neighborhood favorite in Brooklyn has high ceilings, brick walls and an open kitchen. The menu features seasonal fish and locally sourced meat and produce, but the highlight is the Wild Game Festival (winter to spring).

🔲 H22 ✉ 72 Henry Street/Cranberry Street, Brooklyn Heights ☎ 718/834-1776 🕐 Daily dinner 🚇 2, 3 Clark Street; A, C High Street

JACKSON HOLE $

jacksonholeburgers.com

This small chain of burger places is useful when all you want is a hefty sandwich in a child-friendly, no-frills environment.

🔲 F8 ✉ 232 E 64th Street/2nd Avenue ☎ 212/371-7187 🕐 Daily lunch and dinner 🚇 6 68th Street–Hunter College

---

GRAND CENTRAL

Here are some highlights of the Dining Concourse at Grand Central Terminal:
Central Market New York makes creative, delicious sandwiches.
Café Spice is good for curries.
Grand Central Oyster Bar is an upscale seafood bar, with cocktails (▷ 148).
Magnolia Bakery is for great pastries.
Shake Shack has world-renowned burgers plus tasty fat-top dogs and shakes.
Mendy's Kosher Delicatessen has noodle soup, knishes and pastrami-on-rye.

JEAN-GEORGES $$$

jean-georgesrestaurant.com

One of the world's great chefs, Alsace native Jean-Georges Vongerichten is known for his refined, full-flavored Asian-accented cooking. The glass-walled minimalist rooms feel serene and special, decorated in neutral colors. Lunch here is a (relative) bargain, but always book ahead.

🔲 C9 ✉ 1 Central Park West/60th Street ☎ 212/299-3900 🕐 Mon–Sat lunch and dinner, Sun dinner 🚇 1, A, B, C, D 59th Street–Columbus Circle

EAT

Casa Lever

Katz's, a deli to die for

The choices change each month, with emphasis on seasonal dishes. Reserve well in advance.

🚩 E12 ✉ 125 E 39th Street/Lexington Avenue ☎ 212/228-4873 🕓 Tue–Sun dinner 🚇 4, 5, 6, 7, S 42nd Street–Grand Central

JOHN'S PIZZERIA $

johnspizzerianyc.com

This converted church (do look up to enjoy the beautiful stained-glass ceiling) has one of just a handful of coal brick-ovens left in the city. It's a great spot to head to for a pre- or post-theater pizza.

🚩 C11 ✉ 260 W 44th Street ☎ 212/391-7560 🕓 Daily lunch and dinner 🚇 1, 2, 3, 7, N, Q, R, S, W Times Square-42nd Street

KAJITSU $$$

kajitsunyc.com

The only vegetarian restaurant in New York to be awarded a Michelin star, Kajitsu promotes Japanese *shojin* cuisine through its multi-course tasting menus.

KATZ'S DELI $

katzsdelicatessen.com

Visited by thousands each week, this is the site of the famous climactic scene in *When Harry Met Sally*. It's also the last deli in a once thriving Jewish neighborhood. Opened in 1888, it upholds traditions such as plain surroundings, and serves knishes and pastrami sandwiches.

🚩 G17 ✉ 205 E Houston Street/Ludlow Street ☎ 212/254-2246 🕓 Daily breakfast, lunch and dinner 🚇 F 2nd Avenue

THE LOEB BOATHOUSE $$

thecentralparkboathouse.com

Leave hectic Manhattan behind at this lakeside place in Central Park. The food is contemporary American but the view is the main reason for coming. The cocktail deck gets busy in summer. Reservations are advised.

🚩 D7 ✉ Central Park, nearest to E 72nd Street entrance ☎ 212/517-2233 🕓 Mon–Fri lunch and dinner, Sat–Sun brunch and dinner, lunch only Dec–Mar 🚇 6 68th Street–Hunter College

NEW YORK RESTAURANT WEEK

The best dining deal in town is no longer a mere seven-day affair. New York Restaurant Week now takes place twice a year, and lasts for up to a month each winter and summer. Participating restaurants offer three-course lunches and dinners at a set price. The cost of your drinks, tax and tip are extra. This event offers a great chance to dine at some of New York's best and hottest restaurants for a fraction of the normal price. The menus are designed to show off their classic dishes and cooking styles. Check out the dates and restaurants at nycgo.com, and book ahead—the best tables go fast!

MANHATTA $$$

manhattarestaurant.com

This 60th floor dazzler at the Liberty building from Danny Meyer offers fine American fare plus one of the city's most eye-boggling views. If the tab is too steep, visit the bar instead.

🔲 F22 ✉ 28 Liberty Street/William Street ☎ 212/230-5788 🕐 Daily lunch, dinner 🚇 2/3, 4/5, A/C Fulton Street

MISSION CHINESE FOOD $$$

missionchinesefood.com

This is chef Danny Bowien's NYC branch of the much-loved San Franciscan restaurant. Its current home came with a built-in pizza oven, so Bowien added the Italian staple to his menu of mostly northern Chinese cuisine. It's just a typical example of how this place bends the rules. Reservations are only accepted online.

🔲 G19 ✉ 171 East Broadway/Essex Street ☎ 917/376-5660 🕐 Daily dinner 🚇 F East Broadway; J, M, Z Essex Street

MOMOFUKU SSÄM BAR $$

ssambar.momofuku.com

This Korean eatery is part of chef David Chang's Momofuku empire. The daily menu could offer anything from mason jars of kimchi to slow-roasted pork or pork chops in Asian fish sauce.

🔲 F16 ✉ 207 2nd Avenue/13th Street ☎ 212/254-3500 🕐 Daily dinner, Mon–Fri lunch, Sat–Sun brunch 🚇 L 3rd Avenue

NOBU FIFTY SEVEN $$$

noburestaurants.com

It is difficult to get a reservation at this huge Japanese restaurant, part owned by Robert de Niro, but you'll be rewarded by memorable food and polished wood and

SWEET TREATS

Treat yourself to city favorites like frozen hot chocolate or ice cream concoctions at Serendipity 3 (🔲 225 E 60th/2nd Avenue, ☎ 212/838-3351), Austrian pastries at Café Sabarsky (Neue Gallery ▷ 70) or chocolate pizza at Max Brenner (🔲 841 Broadway/13th Street, ☎ 646/467-8803).

chandeliers. Choose the Kobe-style Wagyu beef, or toro tartare with caviar.

🔲 D19 ✉ 40 West 57th Street/between 5th and 6th avenues ☎ 212/757-3000 🕐 Daily lunch and dinner 🚇 57th Street

NORTH SQUARE $$

northsquareny.com

Chef Yoel Cruz's inventive cooking focuses on European and Asian-influenced dishes. The atmosphere is relaxed, and dishes such as coriander-crusted yellowfin tuna are sublime. The Sunday jazz brunch has sets at 12.30 and 2.15.

🔲 D16 ✉ 103 Waverly Place/MacDougal Street ☎ 212/254-1200 🕐 Daily breakfast and dinner, Mon–Fri lunch, Sat–Sun brunch 🚇 A, B, C, D, E, F, M West 4th Street–Washington Square

THE ODEON $$

theodeonrestaurant.com

The original hot spot of the Bright Lights, Big City age of the 1980s, this art deco-style restaurant is still going strong. Its tiled floors, dim lighting and happy bar area are some reasons why—that and the always-reliable nouvelle American food, including all-day breakfast that is served through the late night.

🔲 D20 ✉ 145 West Broadway/Thomas Street ☎ 212/233-0507 🕐 Daily breakfast, lunch and dinner 🚇 A, C Chambers Street

ORIENTAL GARDEN $–$$

orientalgardenny.com

There are several good reasons to visit this big, long-time Cantonese favorite in Chinatown: tasty dim sum, seafood fresh from the tanks, and very good prices.

✚ F19 ✉ 14 Elizabeth Street/Bayard Canal ☎ 212/619-0085 ◉ Daily lunch and dinner 🚇 6, J, N, R, Q Canal Street

OYSTER BAR $$

oysterbarny.com

This 1913 vaulted room in Grand Central Terminal is a must if you're looking for a quintessential New York experience. There's plenty on the menu to choose from, including fish and shellfish.

✚ E11 ✉ Grand Central Terminal, lower level ☎ 212/490-6650 ◉ Mon–Sat lunch and dinner 🚇 4, 5, 6, 7 Grand Central–42nd Street

PER SE $$$

perseny.com

Reserve *way* ahead for Thomas Keller's distinctive (and expensive) tasting menus, including dishes such as hand-cut tagliatelle with truffles, and charcoal-grilled Wagyu. Enjoy great Central Park views with your meal.

✚ C9 ✉ Time Warner Center, 10 Columbus Circle, 4th floor/60th Street ☎ 212/823-9335 ◉ Daily dinner, Fri–Sun lunch 🚇 1, A, B, C, D 59th Street–Columbus Circle

PERSEPOLIS $$

persepolisnewyork.com

This homely, friendly restaurant serves some of the city's finest Middle Eastern cuisine. Try the delicious Persian dishes such as saffron-marinated rack of lamb, and traditional *koresht* (stews).

✚ F7 ✉ 1407 2nd Avenue/73rd Street ☎ 212/535-1100 ◉ Daily lunch and dinner 🚇 6 68th Street–Hunter College

PETER LUGER STEAK HOUSE $$$

peterluger.com

This unpretentious steakhouse has been serving the city's best beef to New Yorkers since 1887. Order hash browns and creamed spinach to accompany your steak. Reserve early. Only cash or US debit cards are accepted; credit cards aren't.

✚ Off map ✉ 178 Broadway/Driggs Avenue, Brooklyn ☎ 718/387-7400 ◉ Daily lunch and dinner 🚇 J, Z Marcy Avenue

PONDICHERI $$

pondicheri.com

Star Houston chef Anita Jaisinghani brings her famed Indian cooking to the Big Apple. During the day, expect authentic street food and Mumbai-style sandwiches; at night, enjoy traditional *thali*.

✚ E14 ✉ 15 West 27th Street ☎ 646/878-4375 ◉ Daily breakfast, lunch and dinner 🚇 R, W 28th Street

---

FOOD ON WHEELS

The lowly hot dog stand and pretzel cart have stepped up a notch. More than 3,000 gourmet food trucks now ply the streets of Manhattan, serving up a variety of tasty, healthy and inexpensive fare to busy New Yorkers on the go. Doling out everything from biryanis to Korean BBQ, organic salads to schnitzel and Belgian waffles, some have reached near-cult status. Trucks broadcast their locations to fans on Twitter, and there are websites and apps to help. One source is roaminghunger.com.

RIVER CAFÉ $$$

rivercafe.com

For a special occasion (jackets required, guys) and drop-dead views across the East River to Manhattan, this is a treat. Classic international food ranges from wild shrimp and rock lobster to rabbit with ricotta.

🚹 Off map ✉ 1 Water Street (under the Brooklyn Bridge) ☎ 718/522-5200 🕐 Mon–Fri breakfast and dinner, Sat lunch and dinner, Sun brunch and dinner 🚇 2, 3 Clark Street; A, C High Street

ROSA MEXICANO $$

rosamexicano.com

Popular with theater-goers, the food seved here is traditional Mexican. The interior, designed by David Rockwell, is contemporary and includes a 30ft (9m) blue-tiled wall of water.

🚹 C8 ✉ 61 Columbus Avenue/62nd Street ☎ 212/977-7700 🕐 Mon–Fri lunch, daily dinner, Sat–Sun brunch 🚇 1, A, B, C, D 59th Street–Columbus Circle

SARGE'S DELICATESSEN $-$$

sargesdeli.com

One of the last survivors of New York's once-famous Jewish delis, Sarge has been serving mile-high sandwiches, nourishing soups and a heaped helping of old-time atmosphere since 1964. It's open 24 hours a day.

🚹 F12 ✉ 548 3rd Avenue/36-37th streets ☎ 212/679-0442 🕐 Daily breakfast, lunch, dinner 🚇 6 33rd Street

UNCLE NICK'S $$

unclenicksgreekcuisine.com

A fun atmosphere and hearty cooking are hallmarks at this West Side Greek restaurant. The location near the theater district makes this

---

BAGEL PEOPLE

If NYC has a signature food, it might be the bagel. One top choice is Tal Bagels (🚹 B4 ✉ 2446 Broadway/91st Street ☎ 212/712-0171), which serves classic flavors such as sesame, pumpernickel and poppy. To go truly old-school, visit Kossar's Bialys (🚹 G18 ✉ 367 Grand Street/Essex Street ☎ 212/473-4810), the only kosher purveyor of these oniony bagel-like breads still operating on the Lower East Side.

---

a popular choice for those looking for pre-performance dining.

🚹 B10 ✉ 747 9th Avenue/50th Street ☎ 212/245-7992 🕐 Daily lunch and dinner 🚇 C, E 50th Street

UNION SQUARE CAFÉ $$$

unionsquarecafe.com

The first of Danny Meyer's growing restaurant empire is one of the best, with a combination of award-winning contemporary American fare and warm ambience rarely found at this level. Note there is, famously, no tipping; hospitality is included in the price.

🚹 E15 ✉ 101 E 19th Street/Park Avenue South ☎ 212/273-4020 🕐 Daily dinner, Mon–Fri lunch, Sat–Sun brunch 🚇 4, 5, 6, L, N, Q, R 14th Street

VESELKA $

veselka.com

Veselka has been a favorite for budget dining in the East Village since 1954. Dine here at any time of day or night on traditional Ukrainian and soul food. The menu ranges from handmade *pierogi* (dumplings) to goulash.

🚹 F16 ✉ 144 2nd Avenue/E 9th Street ☎ 212/228-9682 🕐 Daily 24 hours 🚇 6 Astor Place; F 2nd Avenue; R, W 8th Street

Sleep

New York has a great range of places to stay, with options to suit all tastes and budgets. In this section, establishments are listed alphabetically.

SLEEP

Introduction

New York has hundreds of hotels, but, like most major cities, prices are high and spaces are tight. Here are some tips to help you choose wisely.

What to Expect

In a city where space is at a premium, your room may be smaller than you had hoped but there is no shortage of amenities. Most budget hotels offer private baths, TV and air conditioning, hair dryers and coffee makers. Many have a fitness facility. In luxury hotels, you can expect daily newspapers, robes, spas, room service and a concierge to make reservations and help you navigate the city.

Do the Research

Finding comfortable affordable lodgings is a challenge. Make use of discounted reservation sites like trivago.com or kayak.com, which compare prices from several sites. Rates are usually lower on weekends when business travelers go home. Hotel websites often offer discounts if you reserve for three days or more and may have seasonal specials and weekend packages. When calculating costs, remember that quoted rates usually do not include taxes, which will add about 15 percent to your bill.

Some Saving Tips

Airbnb.com, bedandbreakfast.com and similar services are a growing option. Some also offer apartments, which are good deals for families. Look for hotels with complimentary breakfast and evening meal. And free WiFi is a bonus.

HOME AWAY FROM HOME

One way to stretch your travel budget is to consider a home stay or apartment swap. HomeExchange.com (for a fee) will help you swap homes with New Yorkers. VRBO.com is another reputable source for short-term apartment rentals.

From top: The Plunge Bar and Lounge at Hotel Gansevoort; guest room in the Shoreham; Crosby Street Hotel; The New York Edition lobby

SLEEP

Directory

LOWER MANHATTAN
Mid-Range
Off Soho Suites
Luxury
Crosby Street Hotel
Wagner at the Battery

DOWNTOWN AND CHELSEA
Budget
Carlton Arms
Hotel 17
Mid-Range
Maritime Hotel
Washington Square
Luxury
Hotel Gansevoort
The Inn at Irving Place

MIDTOWN
Budget
Ameritania Hotel
Hotel Wolcott
Pod 51
Mid-Range
Casablanca

citizenM
Hotel Eventi
The Hudson
Iberostar 70 Park Avenue
Library Hotel
Millennium Times Square
The Shoreham
The Time
Luxury
Four Seasons
Mandarin Oriental
The New York Edition
The Plaza
St. Regis

UPPER WEST SIDE
Budget
Hotel Belleclaire
Mid-Range
Excelsior
Hotel Beacon

FARTHER AFIELD
Luxury
1 Hotel Brooklyn Bridge

Sleeping A–Z

PRICES	
Prices are approximate and based on a double room for one night.	
$$$	over $450
$$	$251–$450
$	$150–$250

1 HOTEL BROOKLYN BRIDGE $$$
1hotels.com
This stylish boutique hotel in DUMBO (Down Under the Manhattan Bridge Overpass) has expansive waterfront views of the East River and Manhattan skyline.

It was designed by local artists, and there's also a rooftop pool.
🚇 Off map ✉ 60 Furman Street
☎ 347/696-2500 🚇 A, C High Street, F York Street

AMERITANIA HOTEL $$
ameritanianyc.com
If you want to be in the heart of the theater district then this Times Square hotel in a Beaux Arts building, provides mid-class accommodations with spacious common areas and lounge bar.
🚇 C10 ✉ 230 W 54th Street/Broadway
☎ 212/247-5000 🚇 N, Q, R, W 57th Street–7th Avenue

SLEEP

CARLTON ARMS $

carltonarms.com

Decorated with crazy murals in the lobby and some rooms, this is one of New York's wackiest hotels, close to Madison Square. Amenities are minimal but there is a communal, boho atmosphere that makes visitors feel at home. As it says on the business card, "this ain't no Holiday Inn."

F14 ✉ 160 E 25th Street/Lexington–3rd avenues ☎ 212/679-0680 6 23rd Street

CASABLANCA $$

casablancahotel.com

Moroccan prints and tiles make this small, family-owned boutique hotel an oasis of color and style. Rooms range from cozy classics to premium kings and mini-suites, all with luxurious bath amenities and complimentary WiFi. Deluxe continental breakfast and passes to New York Sports Club are included in your stay.

D11 ✉ 147 W 43rd Street/7th Avenue ☎ 212/869-1212 1, 2, 3, 7, N, Q, R, S, W Times Square–42nd Street

CITIZENM $–$$

citizenm.com

Mood pads—high-tech controls in rooms that manage the lights, TV and window blinds—are among many reasons visitors come to this happening Dutch import. A rooftop bar just for guests, a state-of-the-art 20th-floor gym with views and a big jazzy living-room lobby with a 24-hour bar/café add to the attractions. The rooms are as tight as a ship's cabin but with king-size beds. WiFi and movies are free; join the citizenM Club to receive room discounts.

D10 ✉ 218 W 50th Street ☎ 212/461-3638 1, C, E 50th Street

CROSBY STREET HOTEL $$$

crosbystreethotel.com

Located in the heart of vibrant SoHo, the 86 rooms and suites over 11 floors have full-length warehouse-style windows. The interior design by Kit Kemp is fresh and contemporary, and the hotel has a gym, cinema and a sculpture garden, as well as a selection of one- and two-bedroom suites.

The bar in Crosby Street Hotel, a fashionable choice in SoHo

The Ty Warner Penthouse in the Four Seasons

⊞ E18 ✉ 79 Crosby Street, between Prince and Spring streets ☎ 212/226-6400 🚇 4, 6 Spring Street–Lafayette Street

EXCELSIOR $$

excelsiorhotelny.com

The location is fabulous—just a few steps from Central Park and the American Museum of Natural History. The building is old-fashioned, with wood paneling, faux-oils and gilt frames. Rooms, though not beautiful, are fine, especially the standard rooms that overlook the park.

⊞ C6 ✉ 45 W 81st Street/Columbus ☎ 212/362-9200 🚇 B, C 81st Street–Museum of Natural History

FOUR SEASONS $$$

fourseasons.com/newyork

The grandiose I.M. Pei building makes a big first impression—all towering lobbies, marble and mezzanine lounges, plus the Ty Bar. The rooms don't disappoint. They're big, with tons of closets, tubs that fill in no time and, in some, great views. Many consider this Manhattan's top hotel.

⊞ E9 ✉ 57 E 57th Street, Park–Madison avenues ☎ 212/758-5700 🍴 The Garden, TY Bar 🚇 N, R 5th Avenue

HOTEL 17 $

hotel17ny.com

The kitschy decor almost seems deliberate—its stripy wallpaper and floral bedspreads seem to hit a chord with fashionable types. That could also be on account of its brownstone Gramercy Park location and low rates, plus free WiFi and coffee machines. All rooms have shared bathrooms.

⊞ F15 ✉ 225 E 17th Street/2nd–3rd avenues ☎ 212/475-2845 🚇 L 3rd Avenue

HOTEL BEACON $$

beaconhotel.com

Set in the middle of Broadway, on the Upper West Side, the Beacon feels more like an apartment building than a hotel. All rooms here have kitchenettes, plus free WiFi.

⊞ B7 ✉ 2130 Broadway/75th Street ☎ 212/787-1100 🚇 1, 2, 3 72nd Street

HOTEL BELLECLAIRE $$

hotelbelleclaire.com

Mark Twain lived here, as did Maxim Gorky, and Babe Ruth was a notable guest. This early 20th-century building offers nicely decorated guest rooms that maintain some of their historic charm, while being thoroughly modern.

⊞ B6 ✉ 250 W 77th Street/Broadway ☎ 212/362-7700 🚇 1 79th Street

HOTEL EVENTI $$

hoteleventi.com

This stylish Chelsea hotel has a hospitable sitting room-lobby where morning coffee and evening wine are offered. Rooms have contemporary decor, floor-to-ceiling windows for city views and rainfall

SLEEP

B&BS

To live like a local, stay in a B&B, of which there are plenty in all five boroughs. Often located in historic brownstones in charming neighborhoods, many offer great prices and the quality of the rooms can be as good if not better than some hotels. Be aware, however, that some B&Bs don't actually include the second B, breakfast, and be sure to be near a subway stop. Visit bedandbreakfast.com or airbnb.com for listings.

Rooftop pool at Hotel Gansevoort

showers in the marble bathrooms. The Vine bar, with a 24-hour menu and L'Amico, an Italian restaurant, are on the premises.
➕ D13 ✉ 851 6th Avenue/29th Street ☎ 212/564-4567 🚇 1 28th Street; F 34th Street

HOTEL GANSEVOORT $$$
hotelgansevoort.com
A stylish hotel that's packed with facilities, including a rooftop pool, a spa, the Chester restaurant and bar, and the rooftop bar and lounge. The guest rooms are furnished in stone and sand colors and equipped with high-tech gadgets. There's a sister hotel on Park Avenue.
➕ C16 ✉ 18 9th Avenue/13th Street ☎ 212/206-6700 🚇 A, C, E 14th Street; L 8th Avenue

HOTEL WOLCOTT $$
wolcott.com
Within walking distance of the Empire State Building, this hotel has comfortable rooms with private bath, plus free breakfast and a fitness center.
➕ D13 ✉ 4 W 31st Street, between 5th Avenue and Broadway ☎ 212/268-2900 🚇 B, D, F, M, N, Q, R, W 34th Street–Herald Square

THE HUDSON $$
hudsonhotel.com
All subdued lighting and minimalist chic, the Hudson is close to Central Park. It comes alive at night with a popular cocktail bar and lounge, and there's a rooftop terrace and a basement gym. Request a room (tiny, even by NY standards) overlooking the atrium, as these tend to be much quieter.
➕ B9 ✉ 358 W 58th Street/Columbus Avenue ☎ 212/554-6000 🚇 1, A, B, C, D 59th Street–Columbus Circle

IBEROSTAR 70 PARK AVENUE $$
iberostar.com
This large hotel in Midtown's Murray Hill has a quietly contemporary decor, luxurious extras such as touch-screen room service, a pillow menu, good sound systems and a 24-hour fitness center.
➕ E12 ✉ 70 Park Avenue/38th Street ☎ 212/973-2400 🍴 Silverleaf Tavern 🚇 4, 5, 6, 7, S Grand Central–42nd Street

LOCATION, LOCATION, LOCATION

Thinking about how you plan to spend your time in New York can help you find the best neighborhood in which to stay. Planning several trips to the theater? A hotel within walking distance of Times Square will be a real plus. Love people-watching? The Upper West Side is great for strolling and its hotels are within easy reach of Central Park. Shopping? Check out a Lower Manhattan hotel near SoHo's many stores.

THE INN AT IRVING PLACE $$$

innatirving.com

This discreet hotel (there's no name outside) is set in two 1830s town houses near Gramercy Park, with elegant decor, period furniture and open fireplaces. The intimate size and period styling make you feel as if you've stepped into a Merchant Ivory film.

➕ E15 ✉ 56 Irving Place/17th Street ☎ 212/533-4600 🚇 4, 5, 6, L, N, Q, R, W Union Square

LIBRARY HOTEL $$

libraryhotel.com

Each of the 10 floors of the hotel is dedicated to a subject category from the Dewey Decimal System, and each room has a collection of related art and books. The interior is modern and minimalist. The Reading Room is the venue of complimentary breakfast and evening wine-and-cheese receptions, and the poetry garden is a charming and relaxing oasis.

➕ E11 ✉ 299 Madison Avenue/41st Street ☎ 212/983-4500 🚇 4, 5, 6, 7, S Grand Central–42nd Street

MANDARIN ORIENTAL $$$

mandarinoriental.com/newyork

The Mandarin Oriental, built upward from the 35th floor, offers stunning city panoramas. The best of the luxurious rooms and suites have floor-to-ceiling views looking across Central Park or over the Hudson. The hotel also has a luxury spa and wellness center.

➕ C9 ✉ 80 Columbus Circle/60th Street ☎ 212/805-8800 🍴 Asiate 🚇 1, A, B, C, D 59th Street–Columbus Circle

MARITIME HOTEL $$

themaritimehotel.com

Right in the thick of the Meatpacking District, this is where quirky meets effortless style. Porthole windows facing the Hudson and navy-blue soft furnishings add to the ship-like feel of the decor. Facilities include a fitness center, a happening bar scene and an Asian-fusion restaurant. Guests can also make use of the free bicycles for sightseeing.

➕ C15 ✉ 363 W 16th Street/9th Avenue ☎ 212/242-4300 🍴 Tao Downtown 🚇 A, C, E 14th Street

View over the Hudson from the Mandarin Oriental

MILLENNIUM TIMES SQUARE $$

millenniumhotels.com

Close to many Broadway shows, plus Times Square, the Millennium is a good choice for theater-lovers. The high-ceilinged lobby leads to a 52-story building, with 750 guest rooms, and suites that have floor-to-ceiling windows for great views.

➕ D11 ✉ 145 W 44th Street/Broadway ☎ 212/768-4400 🚇 1, 2, 3 ,7, N, Q, R, S, W Times Square–42nd Street

THE NEW YORK EDITION $$$

editionhotels.com

This luxury hotel is housed in a 1909, 41-story clocktower with jaw-dropping views. Rooms are in elegant wood tones. It also has a flagship restaurant from Michelin-starred chef Jason Atherton.

➕ E14 ✉ 5 Madison Avenue/E 24th Street ☎ 212/413-4200 🚇 N, R 23rd Street

OFF SOHO SUITES $$

offsoho.com

Since opening 20 years ago, this hotel's very off-SoHo location (on the Lower East Side bordering Nolita) has become all the rage. The suites are mini-studio apartments with modern, no-fuss decor, full kitchen facilities, private phones and satellite TV. The economy suites share a kitchen and bathroom.

➕ F18 ✉ 11 Rivington Street/Bowery ☎ 212/979-9815 🚇 F 2nd Avenue; J, Z Bowery

THE PLAZA $$$

theplazany.com

With suites and rooms overlooking Fifth Avenue or Central Park, this is one of the city's landmark hotels.

➕ D9 ✉ 5th Avenue at Central Park South ☎ 212/759-3000 🚇 N, R, W 5th Avenue–59th Street

POD 51 $

thepodhotel.com

Rooms are small but the rates are competitive. Some rooms share baths, while some have bunk beds popular with families. Check the website for other locations.

➕ F10 ✉ 230 E 51st Street/2nd–3rd avenues ☎ 844/763-7666 🚇 6 51st Street/M 53rd Street

The Shoreham's bar

ST. REGIS $$$

marriot.com

Founded in 1904 by John Jacob Astor IV, this hotel offers opulent Louis XV style in the middle of Midtown. It has extremely plush rooms and suites, a myriad of amenities. The service is discreet and there's even a butler.

⊞ E9–E10 ✉ 2 E 55th Street/5th Avenue ☎ 212/753-4500 ⓐ E, M 5th Avenue–53rd Street

THE SHOREHAM $$

shorehamhotel.com

The Shoreham has small but tasteful rooms and suites, with the choice rooms at the back. Extras such as Aveda products, free coffee and a hotel-curated art gallery, plus high-end tech in the better rooms, add good value.

⊞ D10 ✉ 33 W 55th Street/5th–6th avenues ☎ 866/950-8893 ⓐ B, D, E 57th Street

THE TIME $$

thetimeny.com

In the heart of the theater district, the hotel has newly designed rooms by David Rockwell, done in light woods with a clean, modern look. Guests enjoy complimentary breakfast, daytime tea and coffee, evening wine and cheese.

⊞ C11 ✉ 224 W 49th Street/between Broadway and 8th Avenue ☎ 212/246-5252 ⓐ 1, 2, 3, 7, N, Q, R, S, W Times Square–42nd Street

WAGNER AT THE BATTERY $$–$$$

thewagnerhotel.com

This glass-sided tower has views of New York harbor and of the Statue of Liberty. Décor is pale and contemporary. Amenities include continental breakfast.

⊞ D23 ✉ 2 West Street/Battery Place ☎ 212/344-0800 ⓐ 1 South Ferry

WASHINGTON SQUARE $$

washingtonsquarehotel.com

The only hotel in the heart of the Village is a favorite of musicians and artists. The small but smart rooms have retro furniture, while the beautiful lobby has a bright 1930s Parisian air.

⊞ E16 ✉ 103 Waverley Place/MacDougal Street ☎ 212/777-9515 ⓐ A, B, C, D, E, F, M 4th Street–Washington Square

SLEEP

The New York Edition clocktower

Need to Know

This section takes you through all the practical aspects of your trip to make it run more smoothly and to give you confidence before you go and while you are there.

NEED TO KNOW

Planning Ahead

WHEN TO GO

New York is at its best on crisp, sunny days. Summer can be humid, but hot spells generally do not last more than a few days, and the city is bursting with activity. Fall is generally the best time to visit. Winter may bring the occasional snowstorm, but it is the least crowded and most economical season to visit.

TEMPERATURE

JAN	FEB	MAR	APR	MAY	JUN	JUL	AUG	SEP	OCT	NOV	DEC
39°F	41°F	46°F	61°F	70°F	81°F	84°F	82°F	77°F	66°F	54°F	39°F
4°C	5°C	8°C	16°C	21°C	27°C	29°C	28°C	25°C	19°C	12°C	4°C

Spring (March to May) is unpredictable—even in April snow showers can alternate with shirtsleeves weather—but the worst of winter is usually over by mid-March.

Summer (June to August) sees many pleasant days in the 80s, but be prepared for spells of heat and humidity, especially in August.

Fall (September to November) sees warm temperatures persisting into October.

Winter (December to February) varies. Some years can bring cold and snow, while others can be quite mild.

WHAT'S ON

January/February *Chinese New Year* (Chinatown).

February *Westminster Kennel Club Dog Show* (☎ 212/213-3165).

March 17 *St. Patrick's Day Parade* (5th Avenue, 44th–86th streets).

March/April *Easter Parade* (5th Avenue, 44th–57th streets).

April–October *Baseball season.*

May *9th Avenue International Food Festival* (9th Avenue, 37th–57th streets ☎ 212/581-7217).

June *Metropolitan Opera park concerts* (☎ 212/362-6000). *Lesbian and Gay Pride*

Parade (52nd Street and 5th Avenue to Christopher and Greenwich streets).

June–September *Shakespeare in the Park* (Delacorte Theater ☎ 212/539-8750). *NY Philharmonic park concerts.*

July 4 *Independence Day.*

July–August *Harlem Week* (☎ 212/862-8745). *Lincoln Center Out-of-Doors Festival* (☎ 212/875-5000).

August–September *US Open Tennis Championships* (☎ 718/760-6200).

September *Feast of San Gennaro* (Little Italy).

September–October *New York Film Festival* (Lincoln Center ☎ 212/875-5601).

October *Columbus Day Parade* (5th Avenue, 44th–79th streets).

November *NYC Marathon* (Staten Island to Central Park, nycmarathon.org). *Macy's Thanksgiving Day Parade* (✉ Central Park West, 77th Street ☎ 212/494-4495).

December *Tree Lighting Ceremony* (✉ Rockefeller Center ☎ 212/332-6868). *New Year's Eve celebrations* (✉ Times Square).

162

NEW YORK ONLINE

nycgo.com
The official tourism website, linked to the NYC Information Center in Midtown, includes a calendar of events, accommodations information, news updates and lots more. The helpful trip-planning section includes themed itineraries.

broadway.org
The Broadway League's official site, with up-to-date information on shows, theaters and the theater district in several languages.

newyorkcityanswers.com
Want to know what books to read before you get to the city? Which are the best tours? Tips and tricks from native New Yorkers? This aptly named site tells all.

nyc.gov
As the official homepage of the City of New York, the site offers links to the Office of the Mayor as well as information about community services, legal policies, city agencies and the local helpline.

nyc-arts.org
With a comprehensive calendar ranging from lectures about architecture to whether the circus is in town, NYC-ARTS lives up to its catchphrase as "the complete guide."

nymag.com
One of the most comprehensive websites covering what's on in the city, including good restaurant and theater reviews.

nytimes.com
Here you'll get an inside look at New York from one of the world's most respected newspapers. The site has links to sections covering everything from world affairs to sports.

timessquarenyc.org
All about Times Square and the surrounding area, Broadway and its theaters, hotels, dining and current events.

TRAVEL SITES

fodors.com
A complete travel-planning site. You can research prices and weather, book air tickets, cars and rooms, pose questions to fellow travelers and find links to other sites.

iloveny.com
Official NY State site. Information about touring the city and beyond.

mta.info
The Metropolitan Transportation Authority updates you on service changes and disruptions, and answers questions about buses and the subway.

INTERNET ACCESS

WiFi is becoming more ubiquitous in New York (in parks, cafés, libraries and most hotels), but it's still remarkable how many places aren't equipped—or charge a fee. Check nycgo.com/articles/wifi-in-nyc for up-to-date information. The MTA is bringing WiFi to many subway stations; look for the logo as you enter the station. The subways themselves aren't equipped...at least not yet.

Getting There

ARRIVING BY LAND

- Greyhound buses from across the US and Canada and commuter buses from New Jersey arrive at the Port Authority Terminal (✉ 625 8th Avenue ☎ 212/564-8484, greyhound.com).
- Commuter trains use Grand Central Terminal (✉ E 42nd Street/Park Avenue ☎ 212/532-4900, grandcentralterminal.com).
- Long-distance trains and New Jersey commuter trains arrive at Pennsylvania Station (✉ 31st Street/7th and 8th Avenue).

CUSTOMS

- Non-US citizens may import duty-free: 1 liter of alcohol (this is the total allowance for wine and/or spirits), 200 cigarettes or 50 cigars and $100 of gifts. (No one under 21 can import alcohol.)
- Among restricted items for import are meat, fruit, plants, seeds and certain prescription medicines without a prescription or written statement from your doctor.

SECURITY

- Always allow plenty of time for clearing security when arriving in or departing from the US.

AIRPORTS

New York has three airports—John F. Kennedy (JFK) (✉ Queens, 15 miles/24km east of Manhattan ☎ 718/244-4444), Newark (✉ New Jersey, 16 miles/26km west ☎ 973/961-6000) and LaGuardia (✉ Queens, 8 miles/13km east ☎ 718/533-3400). Most international flights arrive at JFK. For details, visit panynj.gov.

LaGuardia Airport
8 miles (13km) to city center. Bus/minibus 40–60 minutes, $16

Manhattan

24km (15 miles) | 16km (10 miles) | 8km (5 miles)

Newark Liberty International Airport
16 miles (26km) to city center. Bus/minibus 40–60 minutes, $17

JFK International Airport
15 miles (24km) to city center. Bus/minibus 1 hour, $19

ENTRY REQUIREMENTS

Visitors to New York from outside the US must have a full passport valid for the length of their stay and a return ticket. Under the Visa Waiver Program (VWP), visitors from most European countries, Australia, New Zealand, Japan and others do not need a visa to enter the US for stays of up to 90 days. For a full, current list of these countries, and any persons who may be excluded, check the US State Department website travel.state.gov, under "US Visa."

All VWP visitors must have machine-readable passports, and all passports issued or renewed after October 26, 2006 must be e-passports containing additional biometric information. Children and infants must each have their own passport; they cannot be included on a parent's passport.

All visitors are required to obtain an electronic authorization to travel at least 72 hours prior to departure. Registration must be done under the Electronic System for Travel Authorization (ESTA™), part of the US Department of Homeland Security. (Visitors who possess a current, valid visa do not need to fill out the ESTA™ application.) Visitors who do not obtain ESTA™ clearance at least

72 hours in advance can be denied boarding or entry to the US. For more information and to fill out the application (in several languages), go to the ESTA™ website: esta.cbp.dhs.gov/esta. Further information is available on: cbp.gov/travel/international-visitors/esta.

There is a $14 fee payable for the ESTA™ authorization for all visitors in the VWP (▷ panel, right). Payment must be made by credit or debit card, or PayPal, when filling out the application online. The authorization is valid for two years from the date of arrival in the US.

FROM JFK
The journey to Manhattan takes around an hour. NYC Airporter express bus (tel 718/777-5111) runs every 20–30 minutes, 5am–11.30pm ($19). The SuperShuttle (▷ panel, right) runs to Manhattan 24 hours a day ($25). To reserve a place, use the courtesy telephone next to the Ground Transportation Desk. Taxis cost $52 plus tolls and tip; use the official taxi stand. The AirTrain to Jamaica (E, J, Z subway and Long Island Railroad) or Howard Beach (A subway) costs $7.75 and takes 12 minutes, plus 35–75 minutes to Midtown. It runs every 5–10 minutes, 24 hours a day.

FROM NEWARK
It takes approximately 40 to 60 minutes to get to Manhattan. AirTrain (tel 888/397-4636) goes direct from all terminals 24 hours a day to Newark airport station, from which NJ Transit operates to Penn Station in Manhattan. SuperShuttle (▷ panel, right) runs a minibus to Midtown 24 hours a day ($17). A taxi costs $50–$80, plus tolls and a $20 surcharge from Manhattan.

FROM LAGUARDIA
The journey from LaGuardia Airport to Manhattan takes between 40 and 60 minutes. SuperShuttle (▷ panel, right) runs a shared minibus 24 hours (cost $20). Services to Manhattan are also provided by Airporter (cost $17; ▷ above). Taxis cost $25–$37 to Manhattan, plus tolls and tip.

ESTA™ ADVISORY

Since the introduction of the ESTA™ requirement and fee, a number of third-party websites have sprung up offering to process the application. These often charge several times the actual ESTA™ fee and are not authorized by the US government. Travelers should be sure to use only the official ESTA™ website, and pay only the $14 fee. A relative or travel agent may submit an ESTA™ application on behalf of a traveler who is unable to do it themselves.

SUPERSHUTTLE

The SuperShuttle is a shared van service that offers efficient and inexpensive door-to-door service from New York's major airports to hotels, businesses and private residences throughout the city. You may have a slightly longer journey time if your stop is at the end of the driver's route, but the set fare can be less than half the cost of a taxi. It is not essential to book in advance; you can simply turn up at the Ground Transportation Desk and wait for the next available shuttle. However, booking in advance online or by app saves time at the airport. You can also book by phone, and ask about any special promotional discounts that may apply: ☎ 1-800/258-3826, supershuttle.com.

Getting Around

● You are unlikely to recover items, but try the following (or call 311, city helpline):
Subway and bus
☎ 212/712-4500
Taxi
☎ 311
JFK
☎ 718/244-4225
LaGuardia
☎ 718/662-5043
Newark
☎ 908/787-0667
Report a loss quickly if claiming on your insurance.

SUBWAY TIPS

● If your Metrocard doesn't work, don't go to a different turnstile or you'll lose a fare. As the display says, you should "swipe again."
● Check the circular signs on the outside of the cars to make sure you're boarding the correct train. Often two lines share a platform.
● Look at the boards above your head to check whether you're on the up- or downtown side and/or on the local or express track.

TAXIS AND LIMOS

NYC–Licenced Taxis
nyc.gov/taxi
Carmel Car and Limousine
☎ 212/666-6666
Dial 7 Car and Limousine
☎ 212/777-7777

BUSES

● Bus stops are near corners, marked by a sign and a yellow painted curb. Any ride costs the same as the subway–use a Metrocard or correct change ($2.75 in exact cash, or $3 SingleRide ticket sold at vending machines only).
● Bus maps are available from token booth clerks in subway stations.
● Buses are safe and clean but can be very slow during rush hour. The fastest are Select Buses. For these limited-stop buses, swipe your Metrocard at the fare kiosk before boarding.
● If you pay by Metrocard you may transfer free from bus to subway or bus to bus within two hours of the time you paid the fare.

SUBWAY

● New York subway lines often divert for maintenance on weekends, especially in Lower Manhattan and Brooklyn. Check the latest information (24 hours) before you travel (tel 511 or 718/330-1234, mta.info/weekender). New York's subway has 27 routes and 472 stations, many open 24 hours (those with a green globe outside are always staffed).
● Visit tripplanner.mta.info for accurate point-to-point subway directions.
● To ride the subway you need a Metrocard, which you can refill. Swipe the card to enter the turnstile. Refillable Metrocards are more economical than buying SingleRide tickets, and you can share the card with a companion. You can top up the card at ticket machines inside the stations. The best deals are weekly or monthly Metrocards, but these can't be shared.
● Many stations have separate entrances for up- and downtown services, often on opposite corners of the street. Check the subway map and listen to the platform announcements to determine if a train is local or express and will stop at your station.
● Children under 44in (112cm) tall ride free.
● Subways run all night, with many lines (such as the 1, 2, 3, 4, 5, 6) crowded until well after midnight. Late-night riders should avoid less popular routes and always stay in the "off hour waiting area" until the train arrives.

TAXIS

- The ubiquitous yellow cab is a New York trademark and, except possibly on very wet or busy evenings, very easy to hail. Your hotel concierges can also arrange one for you. However, they are now outnumbered by cars from Uber and Lyft, which can be ordered from phone apps if you have an account.
- Another option is Via, a ride-sharing service with very economical rates for those who open accounts. The competition has caused taxis to form their own cars-on-demand site for smart phones called Curb—download the free app.
- All taxis now accept credit cards: tips can be included in the payment.

DRIVING

- Driving in New York is not recommended.
- The address of the nearest major car-rental outlet can be found by calling the following toll-free numbers:
Avis, tel 800/230-4898
Budget, tel 800/218-7992
Hertz, tel 800/654-3131
National, tel 800/121-8303.
- If driving in New York is unavoidable, make sure you understand the restrictions because penalties for infringements are stringent.
- In many streets, parking alternates daily from one side to the other, and it is illegal to park within 10ft (3m) either side of a fire hydrant. A car illegally parked will be towed away and the driver heavily fined. Parking is expensive.
- Within the city limits the speed limit is 25mph (40kph); right turns at a red light are prohibited.
- Passing a stopped school bus is illegal and stiff fines can be imposed.

WALKING

New York is a great city for walking. If the weather is dry (if it isn't, umbrella vendors soon materialize), it's far nicer (and often faster) to hike a 10- or 20-block distance than to take the subway, or sit in a cab or bus stalled in traffic. To work it out, figure one minute per short block (north–south) and four per long block (east–west, on cross streets).

OUTER BOROUGHS

Subway lines that appear to be identical in Manhattan often diverge in other boroughs, so make certain you know which line goes to your stop. Every major subway line goes through Manhattan except the G, which serves Queens and Brooklyn exclusively.

VISITORS WITH DISABILITIES

City law requires that all facilities constructed after 1987 provide complete access to people with disabilities. Many owners of older buildings have willingly added disability-access features as well. An important resource is the Mayor's Office for People with Disabilities (✉ 100 Gold Street, 2nd floor, 10038 ☎ 311 (ask for the office), nyc.gov/mopd. The website has information on transportation, theater, movies, concerts, parks and sport. The city's online tourist guide, nycgo.com, has information about accessibility. Broadway guidelines are available at theatreaccess.nyc (☎ 212/912-9770). For Lincoln Center information: lct.org/visit/accessibility.

Essential Facts

The city runs visitor information centers and kiosks around town. The most comprehensive is at Macy's ⊠ Herald Square ☎ 212/695-4400, nycgo.com ⊙ Mon–Sat 10–10, Sun 10–9. Other centers: ⊠ Times Square Plaza ⊙ Daily 8–7, and ⊠ City Hall ⊙ Daily 9–6. Touch screens allow visitors to research attractions and the center offers discount coupons, including for Macy's.

EMERGENCY NUMBERS

● Police, Fire Department, Ambulance ☎ 911
● Crime Victims Hotline ☎ 212/577-7777
● Sex Crimes Report Line ☎ 212/227-3000

ELECTRICITY

● The supply is 120 volts, 60 hz AC current.
● US appliances use flat two-prong plugs. European appliances require an adapter and a voltage transformer.

ETIQUETTE

● Tipping: waitstaff get 15–20 percent (roughly double the 8.875 percent sales tax); so do cab drivers. Bartenders get about the same (though less than $1 is stingy). Bellhops ($1 per bag), room-service waiters (10 percent) and hairdressers (15–20 percent) should also be tipped.
● There are stringent smoking laws in New York. Smoking is banned on public transportation, in cabs, in all places of work, including restaurants and bars, and, since 2011, in all city parks, on beaches and in Times Square.

MAIL AND TELEPHONES

● There are many post offices dotted through the city, especially in Manhattan. Visit usps.com to find neighborhood branches.
● Stamps are also available from hotel concierges or online at usps.com.
● All New York numbers require the area code (212, 718, 646, 347 or 917) when dialing. For all calls, add 1 before the code. 011 is the international dialing code.
● Hotels often levy surcharges for making calls.
● Foreign visitors: watch out for mobile roaming charges that can result in a large bill on your return home; it's best to ask your mobile provider for information on data plans that can be used in the United States.
● To call the US from the UK, dial 001. To call the UK from the US, dial 011 44, then drop the first zero from the area code.

MEDICAL TREATMENT

● It is essential to have adequate insurance.
● In the event of an emergency, the 911 operator will send an ambulance.
● Near Midtown, 24-hour emergency rooms: Mt. Sinai Roosevelt Hospital, 10th Avenue and 59th Street, tel 212/523-4000.

• Doctor-manned urgent-care facilities, open 24 hours daily without appointment, have opened in almost every city neighborhood. Ask at your hotel or check citymd.com for the location of one of the major groups.

• For any dental emergency any time of day or night, contact Dental Emergency Service, tel 888-350-1340.

MONEY MATTERS

• Credit cards are widely accepted. Visa, MasterCard, American Express, Diner's Card and Discover are the ones that are most commonly used.

• US dollar traveler's checks are hard to use outside hotels and currency exchange offices. It is difficult to exchange foreign currency traveler's checks, even at banks, and fees are high.

NEWSPAPERS AND MAGAZINES

• The local papers are the *New York Times*, the *Daily News* and the *New York Post*. All have Sunday editions. The *Wall Street Journal*, once solely a financial daily, now covers the arts scene in New York.

• Pick up the *New Yorker* and *New York* magazine on newsstands; the glossier monthly magazines *In New York* and *Where* can be found in hotels, and both showcase events.

• Monday to Friday, the free dailies *amNewYork* and *Metro New York* can be found in sidewalk dispensers near bus or subway stops in many neighborhoods, and have both news and event listings.

OPENING HOURS

• Banks: Mon–Fri 9–3 or 3.30; many are open longer, and on Saturday.

• Stores: Mon–Sat 10–6; many are open far later, and on Sunday 12–6; those in the Village, Nolita and SoHo open and close later.

• Museums: hours and closing days vary, so it's always worth checking.

• Post offices: Mon–Fri 8 or 9–5.30. Some open Sat 9–4.

• Opening times are for general guidance only.

MONEY

The unit of currency is the dollar (= 100 cents). Bills (notes) come in denominations of $1, $2, $5, $10, $20, $50 and $100; coins come in 25¢ (a quarter), 10¢ (a dime), 5¢ (a nickel) and 1¢ (a penny). Note: American coins are not marked with numerals (for example the 25 cent piece says "quarter dollar" only).

TRAVEL INSURANCE

A minimum of $1 million medical cover is advised. Choose a policy that covers baggage and document loss, and cancellation.

PUBLIC HOLIDAYS

• New Year's Day: January 1
• Martin Luther King, Jr. Day: third Monday of January
• Presidents' Day: third Monday of February
• Memorial Day: last Monday in May
• Independence Day: July 4
• Labor Day: first Monday in September
• Columbus Day: second Monday in October
• Veterans' Day: November 11
• Thanksgiving Day: fourth Thursday of November
• Christmas Day: December 25

CONSULATES

Australia
✉ 150 E 42nd Street
☎ 212/351-6500
Canada
✉ 1251 6th Avenue
☎ 212/596-1628
Denmark
✉ 885 2nd Avenue,
18th Floor
☎ 212/223-4545
France
✉ 934 5th Avenue
☎ 212/606-3600
Germany
✉ 871 UN Plaza
☎ 212/610-9700
Ireland
✉ 345 Park Avenue
☎ 212/319-2555
Italy
✉ 690 Park Avenue
☎ 212/737-9100
Norway
✉ 825 3rd Avenue
☎ 646/430-7500
Spain
✉ 150 E 58th Street,
30th Floor
☎ 212/355-4080
UK
✉ 845 3rd Avenue
☎ 212/745-0200

REST ROOMS

● Department stores, hotels, book stores, Time Warner Center, Lincoln Center, Rockefeller Center's underground concourse and Starbucks are the best places to find facilities. Rest rooms in smaller shops and restaurants are often for the use of patrons only.

RADIO AND TELEVISION
● For cable subscribers to Spectrum, NY1 is the main channel serving New York and will give you access to news, weather and travel, as well as daily life in the Big Apple.
● WNYC (New York Public Radio) on 93.9 FM and 820 AM has news, culture and music items.
● Many TV shows are filmed in New York, from *Good Morning America* to the *The Daily Show*. Go to nycgo.com/tv-show-tapings for further details on tickets.

SENSIBLE PRECAUTIONS
● Maintain awareness of your surroundings and of other people, and try to look as though you know your way around.
● Avoid the quieter subway lines at night and also certain areas of Brooklyn. Areas of Manhattan once considered unsafe (Alphabet City east of Avenue C, the far west of Midtown, north of 110th Street and Central Park) are less edgy than they used to be. Still, keep your wits about you in deserted areas.
● Conceal your wallet; keep the fastener of your bag on the inside; and don't flash large amounts of cash or jewelry.

STUDENTS
● An International Student Identity Card (ISIC) is good for reduced admission at many museums, theaters and other attractions.
● Carry the ISIC or some other photo ID card to prove you're a full-time student or over 21.
● Under-25s will find it expensive to rent a car.

VISITOR PASSES
Two visitor passes offer big savings if you're planning to take in multiple attractions:
● New York CityPass ($132 adults, $108 children, citypass.com/new-york) is valid for nine days and covers six top attractions, including the Statue of Liberty, Empire State Building and major museums.
● With the Explorer Pass (from $94 adults, $70 children, smartdestinations.com), you can choose 3, 5, 7 or 10 attractions from a list of 90 top sights and tours; valid for 30 days.

Books and Movies

FICTION

- *The Beautiful and Damned* by F. Scott Fitzgerald (1922)
- *Manhattan Transfer* by John Dos Passos (1925)
- *The Catcher in the Rye* by J.D. Salinger (1951)
- *Breakfast at Tiffany's* by Truman Capote (1958)
- *Bonfire of the Vanities* by Tom Wolfe (1987)
- *The New York Trilogy* by Paul Auster (1988)
- *New York: The Novel* by Edward Rutherfurd (2010)
- *Open City: A Novel* by Teju Cole (2012)

MOVIES

- *42nd Street* (1933), Lloyd Bacon
- *King Kong* (1933), Merian C. Cooper
- *Guys and Dolls* (1955), Joseph L. Mankiewicz
- *An Affair to Remember* (1957), Leo McCarey
- *Breakfast at Tiffany's* (1961), Blake Edwards
- *West Side Story* (1961), Robert Wise
- *The French Connection* (1971), William Friedkin
- *Mean Streets* (1973), Martin Scorsese
- *Taxi Driver* (1976), Martin Scorsese
- *Saturday Night Fever* (1977), John Badham
- *Manhattan* (1979), Woody Allen
- *The Cotton Club* (1984), Francis Ford Coppola
- *Desperately Seeking Susan* (1985), Susan Seidelman
- *Do the Right Thing* (1989), Spike Lee
- *When Harry Met Sally* (1989), Rob Reiner
- *A Bronx Tale* (1993), Robert De Niro
- *Requiem for a Dream* (2000), Darren Aronofsky
- *Gangs of New York* (2002), Martin Scorsese
- *The Devil Wears Prada* (2006), David Franke
- *Night at the Museum* (2006), Shawn Levy
- *Julie and Julia* (2009), Nora Ephron
- *The Adjustment Bureau* (2011), J.J. Abrams
- *Birdman (Or the Unexpected Virtue of Ignorance)* (2014), Alejandro González Iñárritu
- *Brooklyn* (2015), John Crowley
- *Beach Rats* (2017), Eliza Hittman
- *The Irishman* (2019), Martin Scorsese

Index

New York City 25 Best

WRITTEN BY Kate Sekules and Donna Dailey
UPDATED BY Eleanor Berman
SERIES EDITOR Clare Ashton
COVER DESIGN Jessica Gonzalez
DESIGN WORK Liz Baldin
IMAGE RETOUCING AND REPRO Ian Little

Published in the UK by AA Media Limited.

ISBN 978-1-64097-327-5

SIXTEENTH EDITION

Printed and bound in China by 1010 Printing Group Limited.

10 9 8 7 6 5 4 3 2 1

A05743
Maps in this title produced from mapping data supplied by Global Mapping, Brackley, UK © Global Mapping and data available from openstreetmap.org © under the Open Database License found at opendatacommons.org
Transport map © Communicarta Ltd, UK

Titles in the Series

- Amsterdam
- Bangkok
- Barcelona
- Berlin
- Boston
- Brussels and Bruges
- Budapest
- Chicago
- Dubai
- Dublin
- Edinburgh
- Florence
- Hong Kong
- Istanbul
- Krakow
- Las Vegas
- Lisbon
- London
- Madrid
- Melbourne
- Milan
- Montréal
- Munich
- New York City
- Orlando
- Paris
- Rome
- San Francisco
- Seattle
- Shanghai
- Singapore
- Sydney
- Tokyo
- Toronto
- Venice
- Vienna
- Washington, D.C.

DISCARD